"Dan has produced an excellent resource to assist university students in processing the timeless questions that always arise in higher education. Dan creatively addresses the intersection of science and faith, and he displays erudition on every topic. His decades of ministry to university students uniquely qualifies him to know the questions they are asking, and to efficaciously address them. This book ministers to students with well-crafted discussion questions that engage the reader in a deeper way. Bottom line: *Epic Science, Ancient Faith* is an outstanding asset for all campus ministries concerned with truth."

— **E. Scott Martin,** National Director, Chi Alpha Campus Ministries; co-founder of *The World Missions Summit,* a global missions launching point for university students; author of *Kingdom Authority: Kingdom authority defined and its components.*

"If you've ever found yourself wondering how to bridge the gap between holding your faith and exploring ever-advancing scientific discoveries, this book is a great starting point. While some argue that religion and science inevitably conflict, *Epic Science, Ancient Faith* is an approachable, essential conversation starter for anyone who is exploring the tension. This provides an excellent way forward."

— **Crystal Burkhart**, Training Director, the Alaska Student Partnership and *What I Have* programs; campus pastor, Chi Alpha Christian Fellowship, University of Alaska Fairbanks.

"Stanford students often have important questions about how their scientific studies relate to their faith. Now I've got a new resource to hand them! *Epic Science, Ancient Faith* will help them think clearly and worshipfully about the Word God gave and the world God made. The book has substantive excerpts from primary sources and rich footnotes: it is a solid introduction to an important subject."

— **Glen Davis**, Director, Chi Alpha Christian Fellowship at Stanford University; Christian communicator and blogger at *GlenAndPaula.com.*

"I am a firm believer in this: all truth is God's truth, wherever it may be found. As it pertains to God's sovereignty over his creation, that truth is revealed to us in the Bible, our ultimate source of authority. But beyond that, we learn more about God's world through art, music, nature, farming, parenting, animal husbandry, business… and on. Dan's optimism shines when he writes, 'All truth comes from God, so let us resolve our differences well.' In this book is a roadmap to appreciate scientific contributions while reverencing the Word of God."

— **Harvey Herman**, DSL, Strategic Leadership; National Program and Training Director emeritus, Chi Alpha Campus Ministries; author of *Discipleship by Design: The Discipling of Christian University Students*.

"Without question I will be adding *Epic Science, Ancient Faith* to my recommended reading list! At a time when the culture is making Science into the enemy of Faith, and science itself is being widely used as an excuse for deconstructing faith, this book is a wonderful gift. Having personally studied science at the doctoral level, I am impressed with Dan's ability to develop a framework for faith and science without deifying science or denigrating Scripture. It's a brilliant book—pass it on."

— **James Bradford**, PhD Aerospace Engineering and Mechanics; Lead Pastor of Central Assembly of God, Springfield.

"This a great book for anyone wishing to know *how* to think, rather than merely *what* to think, about issues of science and faith. It is as much about our Christian posture as it is about anything else; about our need for suspenseful wonder, delight, even-handedness with respect to evidence, curiosity, proper reverence for and fidelity to Scripture, proper confidence in science, and optimism. It will help anyone wrestling with the question of how God's *two books* reveal His truth."

— **Iain Provan**, Professor of Biblical Studies, Regent College, Vancouver; author of *Seriously Dangerous Religion: What the Old Testament Really Says and Why It Matters*.

"Should faith and science spark polarizing, mutually exclusive conversations? Dan challenges readers to explore the possibility that nature and scripture can exist in a healthy relationship instead of as a rivalry. Written with intellectual and theological consideration, *Epic Science, Ancient Faith* invites learners into suspenseful, expectant wonder as we study the mysteries of creation together. Excellent discussion guides model how to think critically about real-life complexities. This is a must-read for influencers in the world of academia and the Church!"

— **Beth Backes**, Ed.D Educational Leadership; Lead Pastor of *The Table Church*; adjunct professor, Northwest University.

"*Epic Science, Ancient Faith* addresses the contentious but critical interplay between Christian faith and the world of science. Dan carries a deep respect for Scripture, for science, and most of all for his readers. His approach is creative, instructive, and accessible. Using case studies from active points of conflict, Dan points to foundational principles for any and all who find science to be a hurdle to Christian faith. I am left with a wish that I had found this book when I was young in faith, and also to give to those I mentor on campus."

— **Brady Bobbink**, pastor and mentor to college students for the last 50 years; founder of the *Student Institute of Campus Ministry* (SICM) and the *Campus Missionary in Training* (CMIT) program for Chi Alpha Campus Ministries.

"Over the past two decades mentoring college students, I've come across many stumbling blocks to faith. One of the most common tensions is the false dichotomy of allowing either science or faith to shape their worldview. Dan provides a necessary bridge that helps us to understand how science and faith are meant to interact—not as opposites, but as complements. This is an incredibly helpful guidebook for students, and our ministry will be richer from Dan's insights."

— **James Junior**, campus pastor, Western Washington University; mentor coach, Northwest Chi Alpha Campus Ministries.

EPIC SCIENCE, ANCIENT FAITH

EPIC SCIENCE, ANCIENT FAITH

Essential attitudes for studying nature
and the Bible in a noisy world

D.E. GUENTHER

TRUTH IN CREATION

EPIC SCIENCE, ANCIENT FAITH
Essential attitudes for studying nature and the Bible in a noisy world.

Copyright © 2022 by D. E. Guenther.
Published by Truth in Creation, 209 E. 17th Ave., Ellensburg, WA 98926.

Cover art copyright © 2022 by Amanda Sedy, Wandering Bird Design.

Photos in Glacier National Park copyright © 2010 by D. E. Guenther.

Figures 1.2, 1.3, 1.4, 1.5, 2.1, 2.2, 2.3, 2.4, 3.1, 3.2, 3.3, 3.4, 3.5, 4.1, 4.2, 4.3, 4.4, 4.5, 5.2, 5.3, 5.4, 6.1, 6.2, 6.3, 6.4, 6.5, 7.2, 7.4, 8.1, 8.2, 8.3, 8.4 copyright © 2022 by D. E. Guenther.

Library of Congress Control Number: 2022907124

Publisher's Cataloging-in-Publication Data

Names: Guenther, D. E., author.
Title: Epic Science, Ancient Faith: essential attitudes for studying nature and the Bible in a noisy world / D. E. Guenther.
Description: Ellensburg, Washington : Truth in Creation, 2022 | Includes bibliographic references.
Identifiers: LCCN 2022907124 | ISBN 978-0-578-46617-0 (softcover)
Subjects: BISAC: Religion and science | Christian theology—apologetics

071122

Thank you to:

Becky Guenther, who supported me without question and who added her quiet wisdom to the tone of this book;

Loren Wilkinson, the mentor who advocated for my project at Regent College and knew its usefulness to students everywhere;

Michael Mowry, the ministry partner who encouraged my interest in faith and science by every means necessary;

Chi Alpha Christian Fellowship at CWU, whose students gave input to each chapter in significant and memorable ways;

Eric Wheeler and Crystal Burkhart, the editors who arrived by Providence to give clarity to each chapter;

Amanda Sedy, the creative artist and coworker who lent her skills to the excellent cover art and book design;

Dave Burfeind at Lazy F Camp, who offered a wonderful place of solitude for me to dream about God and nature; and

Dennis Danielson, the well of resourcefulness who responded to each of my Latin translation requests with delight.

Contents

Letter to the reader

"I want to learn **how** to think, not just **what** to think."

These are the words of my college students whenever I ask about science and Christian faith. Surrounded by rigid viewpoints, they want more space to think. Students want to know *how* to think. And I have come to believe students are a barometer for society as a whole.

How do I think about science and the Bible? How should I make decisions about truth in the natural world? These are common questions for anyone to ask. I recognize that many in the Church today have questions about fossils, the climate, the age of the earth, or a diverse array of other issues which simply do not go away. Some are confused about where to start—or worse, feel like no discussion is safe. And others wonder if they have the knowledge to be in a conversation about science at all.

Would you like to read the news, sit in a class, or go to church and know *how* to grapple with a scientific question? Do you want a better toolset for thinking about science and your faith in a noisy, polarized world? If that is you, read on.

Science is often painted as an all-powerful enterprise—a source of truth that one day will supply a complete explanation for all aspects of life in the universe. In the language of literature, science is the *epic story* of our time. Some even say it eliminates the need for other sources of truth-telling about the universe. But Christians also hold that divine revelation is a source of truth—God's presence and activity in the world are fundamental to life itself. And therefore, faith in God draws us into an *ancient story* that is much older than science. Biblical wisdom continues to stand the test of time across many different cultures.

Should we reject science because of its epic disposition? Or reject Scripture with its ancient roots? No! It is hard to argue with the fruitfulness of the scientific method, just as it is hard to argue with lives transformed by faith in God. Instead, we simply need productive ways to understand epic science and ancient faith together.

This is a book about attitudes. This book is not written to promote a typical Christian viewpoint, such as *intelligent design* or *old-earth, young-earth*, or *evolutionary* creationism. Why? An attitude is a posture that increases our ability to see the truth about a topic. In scientific and theological debates, proper attitudes help us to think more clearly. That is what this book is all about: discovering *how* to think so that we can decide *what* to think. If there is a fixed viewpoint on any of these pages, it is simply one that affirms God's deep purposes in Creation, faith in Christ Jesus, and the humble pursuit of truth wherever it may be found.

Multiple scientific and biblical topics are discussed in these essays. Along the way, you will have the opportunity to read two case studies: on 100,000-year ice cores (scientific focus) and on 6,000-year genealogies (Bible interpretation). I recognize that Christians hold strong views on other topics, including paleontology and biological evolution. But this book was written to teach crucial attitudes and thinking skills, not to serve as a technical guide for every issue. So I have chosen topics that are accessible in the space available.

When they are studied *together*, the realm of science and theology is a space of its own. In this realm, we first study each discipline on its own terms; we work to understand its goals, methods, and areas of authority. Only then can we appreciate how the two disciplines work together. To use an analogy, we study the bones and muscles on each side of the elbow in order to understand the elbow joint itself. This is the approach we will take in this book. Theology and science are considered first on their own, then together.

As I learned many years ago, the word *religious* (from *-lig*, meaning link) has a common root with the word *ligament*, the tissue which holds the skeleton together.[1] As created beings, we are motivated by our God-given passions to explore links —to see the diverse pieces of our experience as one supple body of knowledge. I trust this will help us make sense of any conflicts we encounter on the way.

And so… we have work to do! Faith in God inspires us to learn about the remarkable universe that he has created. Ultimately, learning is an act of worship. I believe proper attitudes will help us make the most of what we find.

— Dan

---

[1] I am indebted to Loren Wilkinson (Regent College) for this insight. See etymology of "-lig" at wordreference.com/definition/lig.

How to use these essays

1. Every chapter functions as a standalone essay. They can be read in any order. However, I do recommend reading essays 1–5, along with 8, before diving into essays 6 and 7 with their case studies.

2. I encourage you to read each essay as a part of a group. Crucial thinking always begins with good dialogue. For nearly twelve years I have tested this book with students, and I can testify that learning is more meaningful for the readers who are part of a community. The discussion questions are written with groups in mind.

3. Remember to read the endnotes. Important commentary is often found in the notes! References are simplified for the sake of readability, however, so please refer to *Works Cited* for a complete bibliography.

4. Permission may be granted to distribute PDF copies of a single chapter/essay for discussion. To obtain permission to download PDF copies, please utilize the companion website indicated below.

5. Primary sources are a vital part of each essay. Whenever time allows, read the sources and do your best to think through each concept. Keep in mind that not all sources support the central thesis. They are included to provide historical context and perspective.

6. Broken links are common in the digital age! Whenever possible, updated links will be maintained on the website.

7. Check out the author's Q&A Forum.

Resources

What about follow-up questions? The companion site for this book includes a forum for readers to pose questions. Since I first began teaching seminars on faith and science, I have always made time to talk with students afterward. Often the best insight comes during the Q&A! Please send questions to the site below. While I do not claim expertise on many topics, my focus on faith and science has granted me the privilege of helping others find their direction.

While this book is about *how* to think, many readers will want to investigate topics in more detail. Here are several books which offer an introduction to the typical viewpoints on faith and science (see bibliography in *Works Cited*):

Any book in the *Counterpoints: Bible and Theology* series produced by Zondervan, specifically on science and Genesis.

Science and Religion: A Historical Introduction, by Gary B. Ferngren.

Origins: Christian Perspectives on Creation, Evolution, and Intelligent Design, by Deborah Haarsma and Loren Haarsma.

Science and Christianity: An Introduction to the Issues, by J. B. Stump.

Finally, the list of 'attitudes' is not complete. Although this book was twelve years in the making, a second edition will arrive much sooner! Stand by for essays on additional attitudes that help us address crucial faith & science topics. Until then, let Matthew 22:37 be your guide: remember to love God with all of your heart, soul, *and* mind.

Companion site ➤ EpicScienceAncientFaith.org

1

Suspense:
away from a brittle worldview

Picture yourself a century from now. Consider what it will be like to live in a world where knowledge and culture have advanced at the same pace as they have in the past four hundred years. What will the world be like?

At the dawn of the space age, people dreamed about the future in popular magazines and TV shows like *Lost in Space*. Their fantasies often portrayed a utopia where men and women fly around in jet packs, drink liquid meals, and talk on video phones. Some of these visions have even come true. Other visions never got beyond the cultural limits of the 1960s (my favorite: comically oversized cell phones in old sci-fi movies). These were interesting ways to think about the directions that knowledge could take our human race. They embraced the sense of wonder and hopeful *suspense* that comes when scientific discovery is seen as a work in progress.

However, science fictions then and now are mostly silent about religious beliefs in the future. So I am left to wonder what Christians of the next century will think about science. First of all, what theology will they hold about God and the biblical revelation of Jesus? And secondly, will believers embrace any future science regarding our planet's natural processes or history—or will they hold the same views as Christians today, without change?

The answer to the first question is that future Christians will almost certainly hold the same core theology as they have since the 1st century A.D. Renewal movements have come and gone, correcting the practices of the Church in every era, but the essential beliefs have remained. The key Christian convictions held throughout history are found in various ancient creeds or statements of faith. Here is the Apostles' Creed:

> I believe in God the Father, Almighty, Maker of heaven and earth.

> And in Jesus Christ, his only Son, our Lord, who was conceived by the Holy Spirit, born of the Virgin Mary, suffered under Pontius Pilate, was crucified, died, and was buried. He descended into hell. On the third day he rose from the dead. He ascended into heaven, he sits at the right hand of God, the Father Almighty, and he will come to judge the living and the dead.

> I believe in the Holy Spirit, the holy catholic [i.e., universal] Church, the communion of saints, the forgiveness of sins, the resurrection of the body, and the life everlasting. Amen.[1]

Christian creeds state the essentials: they reflect basic beliefs which are so thoroughly communicated in the

Scriptures, passed down by Jesus' followers, and upheld by Church theologians, that they endure as a definition of Christianity itself. As early as the 3rd century A.D., Christians pointed to the Apostles' Creed as a faithful summary of the doctrines of the Bible.

The answer to the second question is quite different. Future Christians will almost certainly *not* hold the same viewpoints about science as we do today. Why? Perhaps you would be surprised to know that Christians have never agreed on a standard scientific understanding of the world. There was never a detailed cosmology—a description of the structure and history of the universe—that was universally accepted. Even with agreement on the *theological* premise (for example, that the universe has a Creator and Sustainer), there was disagreement over the *physical* details. Over the centuries, theologians of the highest rank wrestled with the cosmologies that were taught by the science of the time—and then they interpreted the Scriptures in light of that science.

In short, whereas the core of Christian faith has historically remained unchanged, scientific understanding has changed considerably. Here are some examples of past scientific beliefs that were held by Christian theologians:

(Please refer to primary sources on the next page.)

1) Saint Augustine, in the Roman world of the 5th century, sought to reconcile the biblical creation account with classical Greek science. Christians at that time were divided as to whether the Scriptures were outdated and ignorant about the natural world. To settle the controversy, he argued that Genesis 1:1–10 identifies the four

basic "elements" taught by the natural philosophers of his day: earth, air, water, and fire.

2) Martin Luther, a theologian of the 16th century Protestant Reformation, was committed to the earth-centered (or *geocentric*) model of the universe that had prevailed for over a thousand years since Ptolemy in the 2nd century. Luther used Genesis 1:6 and 1:14 to reaffirm the ancient view that the stars are fastened to a hard dome in the sky—the *firmament* or *vault* in most Bible translations. He rejected the notion that the earth orbits the sun, once dismissing Copernicus as a fool "who wishes to turn the whole of astronomy upside down."[6]

3) John Calvin, a contemporary of Luther, believed in a similar geocentric cosmology. He, too, defended the Bible against views that the Earth orbits the Sun using literal interpretations of passages such as Psalm 93:1, "The world is firmly established; it cannot be moved." Calvin speculated that God holds the earth fixed in space while the universe spins daily around it.

4) Thomas Chalmers, in the 19th century, proposed that Genesis 1:2 includes a prehistoric "gap" of millions of years that ended with a planet-wide destruction prior to the six days of creation. This "Gap Theory" was an attempt to explain new geological discoveries that did not fit the prevailing view of a young earth. These discoveries included evidence of multiple ice ages, fossils of strange, extinct creatures, and regular alternations between sea- and land-based sediments in the rocks of Europe. Cyrus Scofield popularized the Gap Theory in the verse-by-verse notes of *The Scofield Reference Bible*.

PAST THEOLOGIANS ON SCIENCE

Saint Augustine, in *The Literal Meaning of Genesis* (c. 415):

> One must surely not think that in this passage of Holy Scrip-
> ture there has been an omission of any one of the four
> elements that are generally supposed to make up the world
> just because there seems to be no mention of Air in the
> account of sky, water, and earth [Genesis 1]. It is customary
> among the writers of Holy Scripture to refer to the world either
> by the expression heaven and earth or occasionally heaven,
> earth, and sea. Air, therefore, belongs to the heavens,
> wherever in their upper regions there is serenity and peace; or
> to the earth, with its turbulent and misty atmosphere and its
> thick wet vapors. And, as a matter of fact, this atmosphere is
> also very often called heaven.[2]

Martin Luther, in *Lectures on Genesis* (1535–1545):

> We Christians must be different from the philosophers [i.e.,
> scientists] in the way we think about the causes of things. And
> if some are beyond our comprehension like those before us
> concerning the waters above the heavens, we must believe
> them and admit our lack of knowledge rather than wickedly
> deny them or presumptuously interpret them in conformity
> with our understanding. We must pay attention to the
> expression of Holy Scripture and abide by the words of the
> Holy Spirit, whom it pleased to distribute His creatures in this
> way: in the middle was the firmament [Genesis 1:6], which was
> brought forth out of the unformed heaven and the unformed
> earth and spread out through the Word.
>
> . . . But whereas the philosophers assert that a star is a denser
> part of its orb, we assert with much greater clarity that it is a
> light created by God through His word. Indeed, it is more likely
> that the body of the stars, like that of the sun, are round, and
> that they are fastened to the firmament like globes of fire, to
> shed light at night...[3]

PAST THEOLOGIANS ON SCIENCE   *continued*

John Calvin, in *Commentary on the Psalms* (1557):

On Psalm 93:1, "Indeed, the world is firmly established":

The Psalmist proves that God will not neglect or abandon the world, from the fact that he created it. A simple survey of the world should of itself suffice to attest a Divine Providence.

The heavens revolve daily, and, immense as is their fabric, and inconceivable the rapidity of their revolutions, we experience no concussion — no disturbance in the harmony of their motion. The sun, though varying its course every diurnal revolution, returns annually to the same point. The planets, in all their wanderings, maintain their respective positions. How could the earth hang suspended in the air were it not upheld by God's hand? By what means could it maintain itself unmoved, while the heavens above are in constant rapid motion, did not its Divine Maker fix and establish it? Accordingly the particle אף, *aph*, denoting emphasis, is introduced — "YEA, he hath established it."[4]

Cyrus Scofield, in *The Scofield Reference Bible* notes (1917):

On Genesis 1:2, "Without form and void":

Jer. 4.23–26; Isa. 24.1 and 45.18, clearly indicate that the earth had undergone a cataclysmic change as the result of a divine judgment. The face of the earth bears everywhere the marks of such a catastrophe. There are not wanting intimations which connect it with a previous testing and fall of angels.

On Genesis 1:3, "Let there be light":

Neither here nor in verses 14–18 is an original *creative* act implied. A different word is used. The sense is, made to *appear*; made *visible*. The sun and moon were *created* "in the beginning" [i.e., earlier in verse 1]. The "light" of course came from the sun, but the vapour diffused the light. Later the sun appeared in an unclouded sky.[5]

Thus, multiple scientific theories have come and gone in the Christian faith. Neither time nor Church council have settled the conversation. Even on seemingly major issues like the "days" of creation, the early theologians differed. For example, the church father Irenaeus regarded the sixth day of creation as a 1,000-year era from Adam to Christ. Whereas Augustine—whose writings on sin and redemption are foundational for much of the Church today— argued that God created everything in a single moment of time. He viewed the "days" in Genesis 1 as an allegorical teaching device.[7] Later theologians like Luther and Calvin favored a literal 24-hour day. Ironically, as we saw with Luther, they also used their *literal* interpretation of Genesis 1 to defend a geocentric solar system! The Flammarion engraving in Figure 1.1 is an artistic rendition of this ancient cosmology: the sun, moon, and stars are embedded within a dome (the vault or firmament) above a flat earth.

Here is the good news: a scientific interpretation of Genesis was never inserted into the creeds. Perhaps the Church Fathers were very wise (or very unconcerned?) with the matter. The creeds reaffirm our core beliefs about God, humankind, sin, salvation, and the Church. But they do not speak to the sciences.

Regrettably—and here is the bad news—Christians in every historical era have used Scripture to endorse various physical theories of the universe anyway. This is a pattern of overcommitment which invariably leads to tension.

Tension from a brittle worldview

What I am suggesting is this: although Christians have kept a remarkably consistent belief about God's truth of

Fig. 1.1 The Flammarion engraving (1888) shows a man who is reaching through the firmament. The title reads, "A missionary of the Middle Ages tells that he had found the point where the sky and the Earth touched."[8]

redemption plan, their scientific beliefs came and went with the times. All too often, they tied "God's truth" to a specific scientific view of the world. There is a predictable downside to this approach.

When Christians tie their beliefs about God or the Scripture too tightly to one physical theory of the universe, it is possible that real, legitimate science may change this picture in the future. And then what does the believer do? Pick one theory over the other? Rather than *suspense*—the sense of wonder at seeing science in progress—there is *tension*. He or she cannot eagerly ask, "How will the details of Creation turn out?" but must defend the religiously acceptable theory, or else the theology that was tied to the theory will be called into question.

In this scenario, "God's truth" about nature is held captive to one side of the discussion, leaving the believer in a state of tension about science:

New science   Christians

Fig. 1.2

MAN'S
TRUTH

GOD'S
TRUTH

Tensions over contemporary science rarely have been good for the Church. For example, the new astronomy of Copernicus provoked a major crisis in the 16th century. Medieval theologians gave great weight to the geocentric picture of the universe. The Earth and its fallen inhabitants occupied the lower, baser levels of the universe. Hell was at the bottom (as in Dante's famous poem, the *Inferno*), and the planets and Sun existed in a higher realm of perfection nearer to God. From this viewpoint, theologically speaking, the earth should not orbit in the heavens as Copernicus suggested. Galileo's fervent insistence that the Earth does move around the Sun was counterintuitive. At his trial Galileo was ordered to desist. His beliefs were judged "philosophically absurd and false, and formally heretical, for being explicitly contrary to Holy Scripture."[9]

Do you see any parallels between the crisis of Galileo's time and the relationship of the Church toward science today? I believe that there are. What do you suppose are the outcomes for Christians today in a state of tension about a scientific theory? Here are two possible choices:

ABANDON FAITH. Faced with new scientific evidence that has the ring of truth, the religious person must reject errors in the "Christian" science. Faith in Christ is abandoned because God's truth no longer seems viable:

Fig. 1.3

MAN'S TRUTH — GOD'S TRUTH *abandoned*

COMPARTMENTALIZE. Rather than abandon "God's truth" in favor of "Man's truth," the religious person must reject the new science and compartmentalize his or her belief system. The two viewpoints remain in a state of tension, with one held in a private world and the other acknowledged (or ignored) in the public arena:

Fig. 1.4

MAN'S TRUTH *workplace & classroom only* — GOD'S TRUTH *home & church*

In either of the cases above, the rigid ties between our theology and our science may lead to a brittle worldview— one inclined to shatter.

Today, there are numerous tensions within Christianity regarding the sciences. They stem from issues raised, in part, by discoveries in geology (in the 1700s), biology (in the 1800s), and astronomy (in the 1900s). In response to this, a *fundamentalist* movement in the Church began to urge Christians to adopt a highly literal view of the Bible. Fundamentalist authors promoted an alternative "young-earth" science, in which Christian theology is tied to a 6,000-year-old earth history. Over time, the central doctrines of Jesus Christ have become tightly connected with a series of scientific beliefs, as if they were a row of dominos:

> God's plan is to use the sacrificial death and resurrection
> of Jesus Christ to redeem his creation from a fallen state—
> which began with the sin of a real Adam and Eve,
> who were created in a real garden 6,000 years ago,
> and who are related to every human by long genealogies,
> including Noah, who survived a global Flood 4,400 years ago.
>
> Therefore, these facts disallow any signs of an ancient earth,
> or any corresponding time gaps between fossils,
> or any form of evolutionary change between species,
> which is used to justify social Darwinism and eugenics,
> and many moral abuses and false human philosophies
> including atheism—the belief that there is no God.[10]

In this view, if one of the supporting beliefs is disputed, the entire sequence falls. The logical connections make it impossible to talk about age-related investigations in any branch of science without the whole theological foundation shattering. For example, if an ultra-literal Bible reader sees in the news, *Climatologists count 110,000 annual layers of ice in Greenland*, he or she would be forced to think: "That just can't be true. The evidence must be distorted."[11] Even if the evidence turned out to be very reasonable or well-supported, he or she would be unable to change a single viewpoint. For the person who holds an all-or-nothing worldview, such as the one we see above, to entertain real, vulnerable dialogue is to entertain atheism.

Over the years I have met Christians, both scientists and theologians, who are able to reconcile aspects of modern geology, biology, and astronomy with traditional Christian faith. But since other Christians argue quite strongly that *all* of these sciences are corrupted by the "slippery slope" to atheism, an epic tension remains. This is particularly true in our Western church culture.

What is it like for you or me to talk about science with this tension unresolved? I once spent several months interviewing Christian students at state universities about their perceptions of science, both in the classroom and in the Church. Here are three of their responses:

> 1: "Most of the churches I've been in expressly avoided the issue of science versus faith. You have science with facts, and faith which is intangible. Once someone raised the issue and our pastor said there's still a lot of debate on both sides, and that we shouldn't go there because it's something that you'd spend your whole lifetime on."

> 2: "For the longest time, I didn't want to let scientific arguments in because I thought that doubt would undermine the foundation of my faith. I feel like there's this creationist idea that the scientific world has a collective agenda to tear down the Bible. But I don't feel that all scientists through the ages have had that agenda."

> 3: "I feel like most of the arguments that you hear from the Christian side come from a lot of people who aren't very educated."[12]

These students lived with unnecessary worry. Their stances toward the sciences were typical of their church settings and characterized by isolationism, fear, and too many unresolved questions. It seems that some Christians have set themselves up to be anti-intellectual—or to have a crisis of faith. Fortunately, the point of this essay is that we can choose our stance. We need a healthy attitude toward science, a middle ground without such brittle tension.

This middle ground toward science is best described as an attitude of *suspense*.

Suspense in the details

The attitude of suspense is marked by an expectation that careful science will eventually sort out the physical details of nature. Living in suspense is not unlike living in the middle of a dramatic novel: one must trust that the author has the end in mind, and he has given enough guidance for the plot to move forward. In our case, the Author has revealed the core theology to live by, but the Scripture provides less instruction about our natural world.

We have two major reasons to keep an attitude of suspense as we walk into the future. First, human beings are prompted by the Creator to have an investigative spirit. The *Creation Mandate* in Genesis 1:28 is God's commission for humans to know Creation to its fullest: "Be fruitful and multiply; fill the earth and govern it."[13] In fact, as we will see in the next essay, the first act of the mandate's fulfillment happens in the very next scene when Adam cares for the Garden and its animals. We are stewards of the creation—we are to care for, and thus to *know*, the world.

As truth-seekers, we must not be put off by incomplete explanations or potential conflict. On one hand, proper doctrine provokes and guides our science onward. On the other hand, when careful science upends our previously-held beliefs about nature or Scripture, we have even more cause to explore and learn more. With an attitude of suspense there is no fear—only the thrill of discovery. It is no longer Christianity vs. Science, but all of humanity seeking the same ultimate truth:

ALL is God's truth

Fig. 1.5

The second reason that we ought to keep an attitude of suspense is that we are called to witness God's truth to others (1 Peter 3:15). Onlookers often reject Christianity because believers tie God's truth to questionable "scriptural" statements about the physical world. To live in an attitude of suspense means we hold the main message of Scripture tightly, as the Church does in its creeds, and hold other beliefs about Scripture tentatively. Suspense acknowledges that there is flexibility in our worldview.

In his *Literal Commentary on Genesis*, Augustine does get this issue right. Although he speculates that Genesis 1 contains the controversial four "elements" of earth, air, water, and fire, he balances his belief with a concern for the proper use of Scripture. And what is the heart of that concern? It is the Christian example to those who are outside the faith. Augustine cautions believers not to get mired in controversy:

> Usually, even a non-Christian knows something about the earth, the heavens, and other elements of the world . . .

and this knowledge he holds to as being certain from reason and experience. Now, it is a disgraceful and dangerous thing for an infidel [i.e., a non-believer] to hear a Christian, presumably giving the meaning of Holy Scripture, talking nonsense on these topics . . . The shame is not so much that an ignorant individual is derided, but that people outside the household of the faith think our sacred writers held such opinions, and, to the great loss of those for whose salvation we toil, the writers of Scripture are criticized and rejected as unlearned men.[14]

As a result, says Augustine, when a Christian uses a Bible passage to improperly to settle a scientific debate, the non-believer will distrust the Bible in matters of science, as well as in matters of greater importance such as Jesus' teaching and the hope of eternal life! Now, *disgraceful* and *dangerous* are not light words. I suggest that Christians be just as diligent to recognize the role of science as we are to handle the Word of Truth (2 Timothy 2:15). Otherwise, we may damage the credibility of Jesus Christ to others.

Let us reflect a good God to the world—especially in our relationship to science. And let us live in suspenseful, expectant wonder as we study his creation together.

~

How many are your works, LORD!
In wisdom you made them all.
Psalm 104:24

For discussion

1. What is something new that you learned in this essay?

2. What were some typical attitudes toward modern science where you grew up?

3. Augustine, Luther, and Calvin all took Psalm 93:1 to mean that the earth is fixed at the center of the sun and stars. Each was a great theologian who misread the Scripture about the physical universe. How do you think this situation could have happened?

4. What are some 21st century examples of unresolved tension between Christian faith and science?

5. Of the diagrams in this essay which describe unstable or unhealthy faith states, which do you relate to the most? Why?

6. What are some ways that people compartmentalize their beliefs about faith or science?

7. What do you think about holding an attitude of *suspense* toward science?

8. *"In essentials, unity. In non-essentials, liberty. In all things, love."*[15] Do you think this is a fair approach to science for a Christian? Why or why not?

9. Do you think scientific descriptions of the world should be included in Christian statements of faith? Why or why not?

10. What issues or questions do you personally want to work out in your relationship toward the sciences?

[1] "The Apostles' Creed," adapted from Philip Schaff, *The Greek and Latin Creeds*, 45.

[2] Saint Augustine, *The Literal Meaning of Genesis*, 3.3.5.

[3] Martin Luther, *Lectures on Genesis*, Genesis 1:6 and 1:14.

[4] John Calvin, *Commentary on the Book of Psalms*, Psalm 93:1.

[5] Cyrus Scofield, *The Scofield Reference Bible*, Genesis 1:2–3 notes. The Gap Theory relied on a mistaken translation of 1:2, in which "was formless" (Heb: *hayetah tohu*) was translated "became formless."

[6] Martin Luther, *Table Talk*, 4638 (June 4, 1539), in *Luther's Works*, vol. 54, 358–359. Note that most translations of *Table Talk* are abridged and do not include this quote.

[7] Irenaeus, *Against Heresies*, 5.23.2; Augustine, *The City of God*, 11.6.

[8] Anonymous engraving in Camille Flammarion, *The Atmosphere: Popular Meteorology* (1888), 163. Image source: gallica.bnf.fr / BnF.

[9] Holy Office of the Inquisition, "Sentence (22 June 1633)," quoted in Maurice A. Finocchiaro, *The Galileo Affair*, 287–288.

[10] See Henry Morris, *Science and the Bible*, 40–41, for a striking example of this logical sequence from a 'young-earth' scientist.

[11] The GISP2 ice core from Greenland contains this many layers. See analysis in chapter 5. Raw data is available as a download archive at doi.org/10.1594/pangaea.870454.

[12] Dan Guenther, "Reconciling the Faith: Christian Students Who Move from Fear to Engagement the Sciences," in *Proceedings of the Inaugural Faith & Science Conference*, 328–331. The students were undergraduates at public universities in Washington State. Responses have been edited for conciseness.

[13] Genesis 1:28 (NLT). The New Living Translation is helpful for its use of "govern" instead of the often-misunderstood "subdue."

[14] Augustine, *The Literal Meaning of Genesis*, 1.19.39.

[15] Attributed to Rupertus Meldenius, *An Exhortation for Peace at the Church of the Augsburg Confession of Theologians* (c. 1626).

2

Delight:
toward our God-given vocation

Place yourself behind the eyepiece of the first telescope. It is the year 1610, and your name is Galileo Galilei. You point the glass to the sky and are startled by what you see. Jupiter has satellites of its own! The white ribbon of the Milky Way has stars. The moon has mountains; you can even calculate their height by the length of their shadows. Everywhere you look you make surprising new discoveries. When you announce your findings to the world, what do you think will be your biggest challenge?

Perhaps (standing in Galileo's shoes) you might wonder: will others question your observations? Scholars at this time believe that heavenly bodies are perfectly spherical and orbit around the earth—the classical view of Aristotle. The Roman Church defends these ideas as well. So you expect that other people will disagree with your findings. But surprisingly, most scholars do not do this. In fact, a few fellow astronomers build their own telescopes and confirm your observations. Church officials in Rome even allow you to speculate, within limits, about the impact of your new discoveries. The debate is surprisingly open.

Instead, your biggest challenge is quite different: some people refuse to look *into* your telescope at all. Despite the obvious usefulness of the new invention, a few eminent philosophers make no effort to see what it reveals about the universe. They suggest that the telescope creates an optical illusion or that it will cause a headache.[1] Galileo wrote:

> Many times I have offered to show them my work, but like stubborn, well-fed snakes they refuse to look at either the planets or the Moon—or even the telescope. . . . This kind of person thinks that scientific truth is like a book—the Aeneid or the Odyssey— and that you discover it not by looking at the Universe or Nature but, to use their own words, by comparing texts![2]

Today it seems evident that Galileo's observations were crucial discoveries that could not be ignored. So where was the harm in looking? One major factor was that astronomers in Galileo's time based their theories on classical philosophy. For many of them, it was not the telescope but the library that was the primary tool for discovery!

Whether these men were blinded by this belief (or were only responding to Galileo's famously prickly personality), we may never know. But one thing is clear: they missed out on the sense of *delight* that comes from gazing at the stars. Nature was treated more or less as a question for the ancient textbooks. And therefore they never gained a better understanding of our wonderfully complex universe.

There are two important aspects to building a healthy approach to science. First of all, our attitude or view of nature affects what we can learn about it. And secondly, our view of humanity *within* nature affects how we choose to treat it.

Here are some examples of past Christian attitudes toward the natural world:

(Please refer to primary sources on the next page.)

1) Jesus Christ demonstrated an important attitude toward nature. In the Sermon on the Mount, he noted that the flowers and birds, both flora and fauna, are inherently valuable in God's eyes. But he also made it clear that human beings are unique among all God's created things and are given a place of special attention.

2) Francis of Assisi, in the 13th century, celebrated *every* natural thing, whether star, planet, wind, fire, or living creature. These were so intimate and familiar to him that he could thank God for "Brother Sun" and "Sister Moon"—that is, co-members of the family of creation. Francis famously married "Lady Poverty" and left behind his material possessions to renounce a life that was disconnected from the natural world.

3) Lynn White, Jr., in the 20th century, blamed the ecological crisis on an attitude of exploitation, rooted in a Western belief that nature is a *lesser creation* given to serve human wants. White pointed to Genesis 1 as the main culprit, with its inanimate portrait of nature (i.e., one without deity). His 1967 article set off an environmentalist reaction against the Church that continues today.

4) Annie Dillard, in the 20th century, wrote a journal of remarkably vivid nature experiences in *Pilgrim at Tinker Creek*. She presents the natural world as both beautiful and jarring in its wildness. More than a lifeless, lesser part of creation, nature is simply *other*. It is a reflection of God's being and active presence. And motivated by the confidence that God is being revealed, Dillard insists that nature can be understood only by living in it and actively bumping against its mystery.

These four examples indicate a very close relationship between belief about nature and the way one lives out his or her life on Earth. Specifically, one's belief begins with a theology. Everyone has some kind of theology about the natural world—a view about how God, people, and nature are supposed to interact. And everyone lives out their theology in one way or another.

The choice by Francis of Assisi to live closer to nature is a good example of this tight relationship. Christians who care about our physical environment today often look to his life for inspiration. Of course, it is tempting to think that Francis trivialized our human position when he personified natural things. (And the many imaginative legends of Saint Francis preaching to the birds do not help.) But this was not the case. He simply raised nature from the low value it was given in the medieval world of his time. He helped to restore to the Christian life respect for the miracle of existence: a love for all God's handiwork, great and small.

Francis' attitude of *delight* for nature runs contrary to another worldview that Lynn White condemned—a secularized version of Christianity which saw nature only as raw material for human use. White called this the attitude

CHRISTIAN ATTITUDES TOWARD NATURE

Jesus Christ, in the Sermon on the Mount (1st century):

> Consider the ravens: They do not sow or reap, they have no storeroom or barn; yet God feeds them. And how much more valuable you are than birds! Who of you by worrying can add a single hour to your life? Since you cannot do this very little thing, why do you worry about the rest?

> Consider how the wild flowers grow. They do not labor or spin. Yet I tell you, not even Solomon in all his splendor was dressed like one of these. If that is how God clothes the grass of the field, which is here today, and tomorrow is thrown into the fire, how much more will he clothe you — you of little faith! [3]

Francis of Assisi, in "Canticle of Brother Sun" (1224):

> Praised be You, my Lord, with all your creatures, especially Sir Brother Sun, who is the day, and through whom you give us light. And he is beautiful and radiant with great splendor; and bears a likeness of You, Most High One.

> Praised be You, my Lord, through Sister Moon and the stars, in heaven you formed them clear and precious and beautiful.

> Praised be You, my Lord, through Brother Wind, and through the air, cloudy and serene, and every kind of weather through which you give sustenance to your creatures.

> Praised be You, my Lord, through Sister Water; which is very useful and humble and precious and chaste.

> Praised be You, my Lord, through Brother Fire, through whom you light the night, and he is beautiful and playful and robust and strong.

> Praised be You, my Lord, through our Sister Mother Earth, who sustains us and governs us, and who produces varied fruits with colored flowers and herbs. [4]

CHRISTIAN ATTITUDES TOWARD NATURE   *continued*

Lynn White, in "The Historical Roots of our Ecological Crisis," *Science* (10 March 1967):

> Man shares, in great measure, God's transcendence of nature. Christianity, in absolute contrast to ancient paganism and Asia's religions (except, perhaps, Zorastrianism), not only established a dualism of man and nature but also insisted that it is God's will that man exploit nature for his proper ends. At the level of the common people this worked out in an interesting way. In Antiquity every tree, every spring, every stream, every hill had its own genius loci, its guardian spirit. These spirits were accessible to men, but were very unlike men; centaurs, fauns, and mermaids show their ambivalence. Before one cut a tree, mined a mountain, or dammed a brook, it was important to placate the spirit in charge of that particular situation, and to keep it placated. By destroying pagan animism, Christianity made it possible to exploit nature in a mood of indifference to the feelings of natural objects.[5]

Annie Dillard, in *Pilgrim at Tinker Creek* (1974):

> It's a good place to live; there's a lot to think about. The creeks — Tinker and Carvin's — are an active mystery, fresh every minute. Theirs is the mystery of the continuous creation and all that Providence implies; the uncertainty of vision, the horror of the fixed, the dissolution of the present, the intricacy of beauty, the pressure of fecundity [fertility], the elusiveness of the free, and the flawed nature of perfection. The mountains — Tinker and Brushy, McAfee's Knob and Dead Man — are a passive mystery, the oldest of all. Theirs is the one simple mystery of creation from nothing, of matter itself, anything at all, the given. Mountains are giant, restful, absorbent. You can heave your spirit into a mountain and the mountain will keep it, folded, and not throw it back as some creeks will. The creeks are the world with all its stimulus and beauty; I live there. But the mountains are home.[6]

of *domination*. Christians today understand that God's command to human beings to "fill the earth and govern it" implies human stewardship and care, not exploitation.[7] Theologians call this command in Genesis 1:28 the *Creation Mandate*. But there is little doubt about the influence of the negative viewpoint. Have you ever heard the phrase, "It's all going to burn, anyway"? It is the root of a mistaken Christian attitude of domination. Believing that God will "start over" when Christ returns is an easy justification to ignore our responsibility for what we have been given.

Even a secular biologist like E. O. Wilson pleaded for the Church to get this straight: "I suggest that we set aside our differences in order to save the Creation. The defense of living Nature is a universal value."[8] A plea like that should make Christians take notice. This universal value is none other than our mandated call to govern the earth—to treat it well. As stewards we must *live* our theology. Jesus' words remind us: the earth is ultimately God's possession.

Now, if our theology about nature affects how we treat it, how do you suppose that belief will influence what we can learn about it? How will it affect our science? It turns out that this is a vastly important question because successful science begins with a theology as well: of nature as a *creation* of God.

Nature as a *creation*

I think it is important to acknowledge that today, as in Galileo's time, we may encounter cautious attitudes toward science. In the Church, we may also have questions about the role of Scripture, such as: *Can we just rely on what Scripture says about the natural world?* or *Does Scripture outrank science in a disagreement?* or even *Do we really need science?* And in the next essay, we will work to define the boundaries of faith and science more clearly. What I am suggesting here, however, is that modern, investigative science is rooted in a surprising view of nature, which is that nature itself is a creation.

We begin here because it was never necessary to view nature as worth studying at all. First, consider briefly the Greek and Roman culture in which the early Christians lived. They found themselves immersed in ancient philosophies. A common view of the day held that nature was the distorted echo of the divine being:

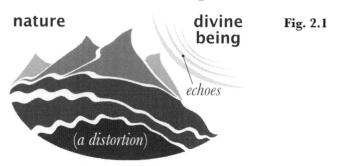

Fig. 2.1

According to a famous analogy by Plato, observing nature is like watching shadows projected onto a cave wall by a fire behind the observer. Objects passing between the fire and the observer cast these shadows. Although the shadows are real, they are merely distorted reflections of the things that move in the firelight. The observer is simply unable to turn around and see their source.[9]

For the many streams of thought that traced back to Platonic philosophy, therefore, the senses were unreliable. Reality (whether "divine" or not) could only be understood intellectually. Thus the Greeks excelled at philosophy and mathematics but gave less time to practical investigation. Studying the natural world would be like studying a cheap imitation of a masterpiece—getting the fine details all wrong. Truth was not to be found in nature. (Moreover, other assumptions got in the way of genuine investigation; for example, Aristotle taught that objects obey inner inclinations rather than generalized laws.) Under this attitude, truly investigative science never flourished in the classical world of Greece and Rome.[10]

A second view of nature is common to many Eastern religions descended from Hinduism. This is the concept of *maya*, the idea that nature is merely an illusion.[11] There are no distinctions between self, others, and objects in nature, because there is only one Reality:

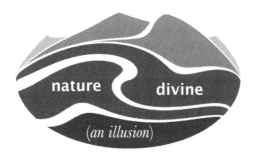

Fig. 2.2

In these Eastern views, nature is simply a part of the divine being. True enlightenment (or *nirvana*) comes when a person overcomes the illusion of distinctions. Practical investigation of nature is unimportant because the natural world must be transcended. As a result, nature has less meaningful value in these philosophical systems either, and once again, investigative science cannot flourish.[12]

On the other hand, a very different idea of nature comes

from the monotheism of the Old Testament, which influenced the development of Western Europe during the Middle Ages. Consider these four verses from the Hebrew creation account in Genesis 1:

> [1] In the beginning God created the heavens and the earth. Now the earth was formless and empty, darkness was over the surface of the deep, and the Spirit of God was hovering over the waters.

> [14] And God said, "Let there be lights in the vault of the sky to separate the day from the night, and let them serve as signs to mark sacred times, and days and years…"

> [26] Then God said, "Let us make mankind in our image, in our likeness, so that they may rule over the fish in the sea and the birds in the sky, over the livestock and all the wild animals…"

> [31] God saw all that he had made, and it was very good.

The author of Genesis describes a viewpoint that is unique to Old Testament belief. Nature as a *creation* is the external expression of God's creative will:

nature   **GOD**   **Fig. 2.3**

(a creation)

Based on the creation account in Genesis, the intrinsic value of nature comes through loud and clear. Most importantly, God considered his creation worth making. And after making it, he gave it his approval by calling it "completed" and "very good."

Two more points in the Genesis account are especially significant for our picture of science. We see that God is transcendent over Creation; he is its source ("let there be"). Also, God created humans to have autonomy. They can act with direction and self-will that are distinct from his own direction or will ("so that they may rule").

Add it all up, and biblical theology leads to a truly remarkable view of nature. Nature has meaning and value because it is a real creation—it is neither a distorted extension of God nor a meaningless illusion. It exists on its own and is an orderly masterpiece of the Creator. And we see that humanity is free and able to act within that creation. Investigative science can flourish under these conditions. Modern science, then, is partially indebted to the Biblical theology of created nature.[13]

Philosophers often use the words *rational* and *contingent* in this context. Nature is *rational* because it behaves according to laws; it is predictable and not fickle. It is like a masterful invention. Therefore we can investigate it. And nature is also *contingent* because it exists only as a purposeful choice of God. In this sense, it is like a masterful work of art. Therefore we can seek to interpret it.

Can we trust that science is able to learn meaningful things about the natural world? Absolutely. This is why the analogy of a masterpiece is useful. If nature is truly God's handiwork—like an intricate Swiss watch, perhaps—you do not understand its inner workings by philosophizing about God or comparing texts. You take apart the watch.

Science as delight in the Creation

In summary, science is built on the belief that nature is trustworthy. The biblical view teaches us that nature is predictable, it is real, and it stands apart as a unique entity. As a work of God, it is also full of meaning and mystery. Most importantly, no amount of reading or theorizing will give us answers about how things actually are. Nature must be investigated in its own right.

This is crucial to our understanding of science. Unless the Scripture answers all of our questions about nature (and I doubt that it does, unless there is a lost book of the Bible), all of the details we need come from the world outside. Our explorations are the real tools of discovery. Our theories must be made hands-on. Therefore I suggest that we follow Saint Francis in the attitude of *delight*.

Our delight in nature comes as a consequence of the creation mandate. That is, our truest vocation is to govern Creation in every good way. Take a look at the words that frame the mandate in Genesis 1:26: "Let us make mankind in our image, in our likeness." God gives human beings a special and unique place in nature, where they are known as his *image*:

nature   **GOD**   Fig. 2.4

GOD'S IMAGE

(a creation)

And what does it mean to be God's image? Being made in his image implies our God-likeness; we possess his recognizable qualities, including personhood and self-will. God's image also implies our representative-ness; we speak and work on his behalf as ambassadors. Francis Schaeffer, the 20th century theologian, describes it in these words:

> We are separated from that which is the 'lower' form of creation, yet we are united to it. One must not choose; one must say both. I am separated from it because I am made in the image of God: my integration point is upward, not downward . . . Yet at the same time I am united to it by the fact that both nature and man are created by God. This is a concept that no other philosophy has.[14]

Humanity holds a unique dual role in creation: we are both God-like *and* created. In Psalm 8:3–6 the psalmist asks the LORD, "What is mankind that you are mindful of them?" And the answer is profound: "You made them a little lower than the angels and crowned them with glory and honor; you made them rulers over the works of your hands." What a fantastic aspect of our theology about God's creation. This is famously illustrated in Michelangelo's painting of Adam (Figure 2.5), who is both a part of Creation yet distinctly in communion with its Creator.

As images of the Creator, therefore, we represent and carry out his divine will here on earth. This realization helps us to understand our mandate in two ways. First, we are given considerable power over nature. As we learned before, we have the power to know, learn, and even control parts of the Creation; but we can also destroy it. Second, we have been made stewards of nature. It is not ours. We must remember its value as God's "masterpiece" and take

Fig. 2.5 "The Creation of Adam," a panel of the Sistine Chapel ceiling which was completed by the artist, Michelangelo, in 1512. The painting illustrates the idea that humans beings are created in the *Imago Dei*, the image of God.[15]

our given place within it. Delighting in nature is a part of our dual role in Creation.

And how can this be done? Returning to the idea of delight, this attitude means that we relish the discovery of knowledge (through science), and we cherish the revealed beauty of God (through our lifestyle). Investigative science is a studied exploration of the unknown that is ultimately driven by reverence. And our natural response is to delight in everything that we discover.

As we read earlier, Annie Dillard's journal is quite striking in this regard. She exemplifies the investigative fervor that we need in our approach to studying the world. It is not enough to read in the Bible that the stars are good (Genesis 1:17) or that the hail and lightning are terrible (Job 38:22–23). As she might say, we must embrace their complexity—both tame and terrible—with our physical senses. Her journal exemplifies the delight of knowing: learning the creeks, the mountains, and their histories; feeling the abundance of life; testing and safeguarding its beauties and imperfections. She writes:

> Some unwonted, taught pride diverts us from our original intent, which is to explore the neighborhood, view the landscape, to discover at least where it is that we have been so startlingly set down, if we can't learn why.[16]

Delight is more than an invitation; it is a guide and a gateway to our actions in Creation. Through delight we are moved to observe nature. And not only to observe, but to contemplate; and to investigate; and to nurture, preserve, protect, utilize, create, and make the most of everything that we discover.

Clearly our mandate is to explore. This is God's design for us. Nature is delightful in all of its ways! And the only way to understand nature is to go outside and look—to exercise our vocation.

When I consider your heavens, the work of your fingers…
what is mankind that you are mindful of them?
Psalm 8:3–4

For discussion

1. What is something new that you learned in this essay?

2. If you had been present when Galileo unveiled his discoveries about the sun, moon, and planets, how do you think you would have responded?

3. Two diagrams in this essay describe unsuccessful views of nature. Do you see any tendencies in today's culture to revert to these views? Describe.

4. Do you think that practicing science can be a form of stewardship? How?

5. In what ways can science be used to glorify God?

6. How might a non-scientist find ways to delight in the details of God's natural handiwork?

7. Are there any limits or concerns that you would suggest to scientists who wish to study nature and "take apart the watch"?

8. Some theologians suggest that the original language in 2 Peter 3:10 implies that the earth will not be *destroyed* by fire but will be *discovered* or *revealed* by a refining fire.[17] How does our interpretation of this verse impact how Christians care for the earth?

9. Read Psalm 8 out loud. How does this psalm change your view of God? The earth? Yourself?

10. What is an example of stewardship over nature that you would like to exercise in your own life?

[1] The men were professors of Aristotelian philosophy: Cesare Cremonini in Padua and Guilio Libri in Pisa; in *Opere* X, 484 and *Opere* XI, 165. See also Stillman Drake, *Galileo at Work*, 162.

[2] Galileo Galilei, Letter to Kepler (19 August 1610), translated by Dennis Danielson; in *Opere* X, 423. Pictured is Galileo's drawing of the moon in *The Starry Messenger* (1610); in *Opere* III, 66. Image source: portalegalileo.museogalileo.it / Museo Galileo.

[3] Jesus Christ, in Luke 12:24–28.

[4] Francis of Assisi, "Canticle of Brother Sun" (1224), lines 3–8.

[5] Lynn White, Jr., "The Historical Roots of our Ecological Crisis," *Science*, 10 March 1967, no. 155: 1206.

[6] Annie Dillard, *Pilgrim at Tinker Creek*, 5.

[7] Genesis 1:28 (NLT). The New Living Translation is helpful for its use of "govern" instead of the often-misunderstood "subdue."

[8] E. O. Wilson, *The Creation: An Appeal to Save Life on Earth*, 4.

[9] Plato, "Allegory of the Cave," in *The Republic*, book VII.

[10] The classic case is made by Michael Foster, "The Christian Doctrine of Creation and the Rise of Modern Science," in *Mind* 43, no. 172 (1934): 446–468. See also Stanley Jaki, *The Savior of Science*, 39–43.

[11] Encyclopædia Britannica: *maya*—"a powerful force that creates the cosmic illusion that the phenomenal world is real."

[12] Jaki, *The Savior of Science*, 26–29.

[13] Foster, 453; see also T. Huff, *The Rise of Early Modern Science*, 46.

[14] Francis Schaeffer, *Pollution and the Death of Man*, 53.

[15] Michelangelo, "The Creation of Adam" (1512), in the Sistine Chapel. Image source: wikimedia.org / public domain.

[16] Dillard, 13.

[17] For example, see Stephen Bouma-Prediger, *For the Beauty of the Earth*, 69, and Susan Schreiner, *The Theater of His Glory*, 98–99.

3

Equity:
balancing God's two revelations

Imagine that God wrote a new letter to the human race. Not in the style of the New Testament letters, but one without human intermediaries, written in his own words. I think many of us would love to have more input on issues that the Bible does not directly address. So perhaps God's letter could be a technical handbook which answers the unresolved questions we have about science or theology. What do you suppose that letter would say?

In my mind, the letter would have a few clarifications about God's nature:

> When you hear the phrase 'Father, Son, and Holy Spirit,' I mean three divine Persons, eternally present in one Being, who share in the work of creating, sustaining, and redeeming the Creation.

It would also give specific details about the physical history of the universe and our earthly home:

> In XXX B.C. I spoke the stars and planets into existence, with light already in-transit to Earth; and after XXX days (or years) I created the continents, oceans, ice caps, etc., with no sign of prior history or age.

And the letter would clarify the human rights situation:

> All human beings should be viewed as socially and politically equal in every way; not only Greeks and Jews, but also Palestinians, Africans scattered by the slave trade, and native peoples of the New World.

Please understand: the examples above reflect serious Church debates at different times in history. They include the doctrine of the Trinity, questions about geological history, and basic human rights.[1] Christians have faced each of these issues in the past. In theory, a direct letter from God would clarify many past and present issues that the Bible does not overtly answer. Numerous heresies, debates, and even bloodshed might be avoided.

However, when we think about it more carefully, God's letter would require constant revision. Many caveats are needed to eliminate every misunderstanding that *might* crop up in the future. Just in recent times, for example, God could have added these revisions to the statements above:

> By 'Holy Spirit,' I do not mean a controllable, impersonal energy like 'The Force';

> By 'planets,' I also include Pluto and the dwarf planets;

> And by 'all human beings,' I also mean refugees who are displaced by wars and persecutions around the world.

New questions about science and theology—requiring even more clarification—will always be asked by people in non-biblical times. In fact, today we cannot even *anticipate* the questions that will arise in the future. This is obviously true for new discoveries raised by our advances in science. So I imagine that God's letter to humanity would be a very long document, indeed.

How, then, can we fully understand God's design for the universe as we practice science? If we do not have a comprehensive technical letter, and if our God-given role is to study the world, what other sources can we turn to? Where does God reveal truth? As thoughtful people, we want to be familiar with any divine revelation that speaks about the natural world.

Here is one option: did you know God has given direct knowledge to people throughout history? God spoke (and speaks) in many different ways, including through prayer, visions, and gifts of wisdom, such as in 2 Corinthians 12–14. Unfortunately, there are limitations in these personal forms of revelation. Spiritual gifts are simply not enough to settle questions about science. No one is perfect at hearing God's voice. And just as importantly, there is no way to reproduce a moment of personal revelation for others. That experience is *not* equally accessible to those on the outside, which leaves us unable to compare notes together.

Fig. 3.1

Thus we need more permanent, and therefore equitable, sources of revelation from God so that dialogue about science and theology is possible between people. And so we return to two primary sources of revelation.

As we know, Christians of every era believe that God speaks to us through the words of the *Scripture*. Christians also believe that God speaks to us, by very different means, through *Nature*. In this way, both Scripture and Nature are a form of "text"—a record of communication—and from the early days of the Church they have been called the Two Books of God's revelation to humanity:[2]

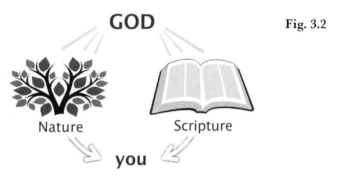

Fig. 3.2

I believe that these two texts can be just as useful as a long technical handbook from God. Why? Because they communicate truth to us as long as we take the time to read them carefully. Words and ideas are *always* understood by their context. And the context of Scripture is a culture that we can study; the context of Nature (by analogy) is an environment that we can test.

These modes of revelation are obviously very different from each other. So let us consider two classic questions:

1. What do Scripture and Nature tell us about God?

What theology, or understanding about God, can we draw from each text? Two passages give us a starting point:

Romans 1:20 — For since the creation of the world God's invisible qualities—his eternal power and divine nature—have been clearly seen, being understood from what has been made, so that people are without excuse.

2 Timothy 3:16–17 — All Scripture is God-breathed and is useful for teaching, rebuking, correcting and training in righteousness, so that the servant of God may be thoroughly equipped for every good work.

According to the first passage, Nature reveals two aspects of God. We see that he is supremely powerful, and we see that he is a divine or supernatural being. Romans suggests that these aspects of God are implicit in Nature (perhaps through the beauty and immensity of Creation) even if they go unacknowledged by any person. As a result, theologians often call Nature the *general revelation* of God.[3]

On the other hand, we understand from 2 Timothy that Scripture is our guide for right living. It gives us a wealth of detail about God's character, the human condition, and salvation through Jesus. Therefore the Bible is the primary text for Christian theology and life practice. Theologians aptly describe Scripture as the *specific revelation* of God.[4]

2. What do Scripture and Nature tell us about how the world works?

What knowledge of the natural world can we draw from each text? Here we have no easy starting point. It is true the Bible contains references to natural objects and events, small and large. But there is no consensus that the Bible teaches us *how to study* the world in a regular way.[5] And Nature, of course, is the object of our study and has plenty to say about itself—if we learn how to read it. Therefore, our main task in this book is to find or develop a way to study the world that makes sense of both revelations.

But this raises a question: how do the Two Books relate to one another? Having *two texts instead of one* introduces an even bigger challenge for our study of nature.

The problem of two texts

Have you heard the phrase, "All truth is God's truth"?[6] Many people believe the "texts" of Scripture and Nature will turn out to agree with each other on scientific questions once we understand them fully. Do you feel the same way? The logic runs like this: God does not lie (Titus 1:2), so his revelations cannot be not contradictory. Although the two texts are not of the same *kind*, we expect to find the same *message* on any topic where they do overlap.

But herein lies the challenge and the real reason for our faith and science debates today: what happens when there is disagreement in our study of Scripture and Nature? Does one Book replace the other? How do we reconcile them with each other? This tension has only increased in recent times with discoveries in astronomy, geology, and biology.

Here are some examples of past approaches to reconciling the Two Books of God's revelation:

(Please refer to primary sources on the next page.)

1) Galileo Galilei, at the dawn of the scientific age in the 17th century, argued that Nature should be understood primarily through testing our senses, not by reading Scripture. Experimental science is fully able to make determinations about the physical world. He famously wrote, "the intention of the Holy Spirit is to teach us how one goes to heaven, not how heaven goes."[11] For Galileo, each text of revelation has a distinct purpose.

2) Henry Morris, in the 20th century, doubted that science was a reliable, independent source of information about the physical world. Because Nature can be interpreted in multiple ways, he argued that Scripture is the only

ON READING THE TWO BOOKS

Galileo, in "Letter to the Grand Duchess" (1615):

> It is very pious to say and prudent to affirm that the holy Bible can never speak untruth — whenever its true meaning is understood. But I believe nobody will deny that it is often very abstruse, and may say things which are quite different from what its bare words signify. Hence in expounding the Bible if one were always to confine oneself to the unadorned grammatical meaning, one might fall into error. Not only contradictions and propositions far from true might thus be made to appear in the Bible, but even grave heresies and follies . . . [So] in discussions of physical problems we ought to begin not from the authority of scriptural passages, but from sense-experiences and necessary demonstrations; for the holy Bible and the phenomena of nature proceed alike from the divine Word, the former as the dictate of the Holy Ghost and the latter as the observant executrix of God's commands.[7]

Henry Morris and John Whitcomb, in *The Genesis Flood: The Biblical Record and its Scientific Implications* (1961):

> The assumption of uniformity [in geology] is one such assumption that can be made, but it is not the only one, and there is no way of **proving** that it is the correct one. The very same data can also be explained in terms of the assumption of biblical creationism and [the Flood], and it is mainly a matter of one's own judgment and preferences as to which he chooses. We frankly prefer the latter presupposition, on the basis of what we consider wholly adequate grounds centered in the revelation of God in Christ. The Bible, as the verbally inspired and completely inerrant Word of God, gives us the true framework of historical and scientific interpretation, as well as of so-called religious truth. . . . We take this revealed framework of history as our basic datum, and then try to see how all the pertinent data can be understood in this context.[8]

ON READING THE TWO BOOKS   *continued*

Richard Dawkins, in *The God Delusion* (2006):

> The presence or absence of a creative super-intelligence is unequivocally a scientific question, even if not in practice — or not yet — a decided one. So also is the truth or falsehood of every one of the miracle stories that religions rely upon to impress multitudes of the faithful. Did Jesus have a human father, or was his mother a virgin at the time of his birth? Whether or not there is enough surviving evidence to decide it, this is still a strictly scientific question with a definite answer in principle: yes or no.

> . . . There is something really special about the hypothesis of ultimate design, and equally special about the only known alternative: gradual evolution in the broad sense [i.e., the universe as a whole]. They are close to being irreconcilably different. Like nothing else, evolution really does provide an explanation for the existence of entities whose improbability would otherwise, for practical purposes, rule them out. And the conclusion to the argument [is] close to being terminally fatal to the God Hypothesis.[9]

Kurt Wise, "Geology," in *In Six Days: Why Fifty Scientists Choose to Believe in Creation* (2001):

> It is my understanding that every doctrine of Christianity stands upon the foundation laid in the first few chapters of Genesis . . . Thus, an earth that is millions of years old seems to challenge all the doctrines I hold dear.

> Although there are scientific reasons for accepting a young earth, I am a young-age creationist because that is my understanding of the Scripture. As I shared with my professors years ago when I was in college, if all the evidence in the universe turned against creationism, I would be the first to admit it, but I would still be a creationist because that is what the Word of God seems to indicate. Here I must stand.[10]

trustworthy guide to all theological, historical, and scientific truth. The Book of Nature can only be understood through the lens of Scripture. Morris co-authored *The Genesis Flood*, an influential book that informed and motivated today's young-earth creationist movement.

3) Richard Dawkins, a biologist and activist for atheistic science, argues that all religions make statements about the physical world. The Bible is therefore in direct competition with the entire scientific enterprise. However, science provides a fully adequate explanation of the universe and leaves no room for God or the Bible.

4) Kurt Wise, a young-earth geologist, says that scientific conclusions about Nature make no ultimate difference to him. In every situation, even if the evidence seems clearly against it, he is compelled to believe the literal statements of Scripture. Ironically, his conclusion "Here I must stand" is a 16th century quote of Martin Luther, whose literal view of Genesis 1:14 led him to defend the notion of an earth-centered (or *geocentric*) universe.

Among other things, these approaches illustrate the real difficulty of holding a "final word" approach to truth. Allowing one Book to define the boundaries of truth for the other Book is like having a marriage where only one partner's voice matters (i.e., "you can have any opinion you want, so long as it agrees with mine"). This approach effectively mutes the voice of the other text of revelation.

Henry Morris' low opinion of modern geology, above, is a good example of this imbalance: "it is mainly a matter of one's own judgment and preferences as to which [interpretation of the data] he chooses." Morris implies that

Nature is wide open to all interpretations. Science on its own cannot be counted on, so we must study the inspired, inerrant Scripture instead. Likewise, Kurt Wise feels he must trust the literal words of the Bible "even if all the evidence in the universe turned against creationism."

To say it another way, Morris and Wise imply that truth about the history of our planet cannot be discovered by studying it directly. From this viewpoint (whether intended or not), investigations of Nature are meaningless and must be viewed as wholly unreliable:

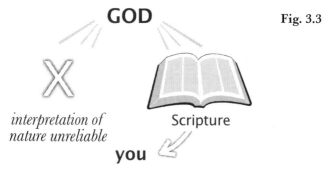

GOD   Fig. 3.3

interpretation of   Scripture
nature unreliable
                    you

Granted, scientific investigation is never perfect. But if a person believes that God's truth is revealed in two texts, not just one, is it possible to blankly dismiss what we see in Nature when it appears to contradict the Scripture?

We see the opposite approach from Richard Dawkins, who denies that any truth comes from religious texts. Whereas the young-earth geologists minimize Nature, he eliminates Scripture entirely. For him the Bible is simply wrong about Nature. And the history of the Church does not help—after all, theologians once defended an earth-centered universe by inappropriately quoting Psalm 96:10, which says: *"The world is firmly established, it cannot be moved."*

As a result, Dawkins and other atheists like him reject the Scripture as irrelevant to science:

(no GOD)   **Fig. 3.4**

Nature   *Scripture is*
                          irrelevant
            you

Is it possible that people at these extremes might misunderstand both Nature and Scripture? Perhaps Christians can trust that each form of revelation gives us real information. In fact, I suggest that we avoid using one text as a final word over the other. Why? Because we are facing a universal human problem of limited perspective.

As many people will point out, the real issue in science is not that Nature's "text" is unreliable on its own, nor that it is exclusively reliable. Instead, our *interpretations* of Nature are fallible. Science is a form of interpretation because it is, by definition, a system of discovery. Science is a human endeavor to make sense of Nature. All scientists are limited by this system—known as the *scientific method*—and by the perspectives they bring to their work. They can err in their conclusions simply because they do not have direct access to ultimate truth.

I hope it is obvious that there is a corresponding blind spot for Bible readers. Again, the real issue is not that God's Word is irrelevant (Dawkins), nor that it is the only relevant text (Morris/Wise). Instead, the plain meaning of the text is not always so plain! Bible interpretation requires technical analysis of the text, often called *exegesis*. Like the scientific method, exegesis is a fully human endeavor—a disciplined approach to making sense of Scripture. When a person declares "God's Word says" they have already taken a step of interpretation. And all people are limited by the perspectives they bring to the Bible. They can err because no one has direct access to the mind of God.

That is why Galileo's approach is a better place to begin. Through the scientific method and biblical exegesis, we aim to give both texts of revelation their due:

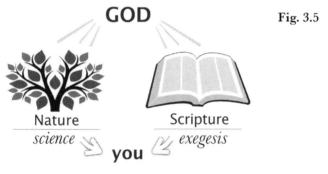

GOD   **Fig. 3.5**

Nature   Scripture
science   *exegesis*
you

We acknowledge our limited perspective by recognizing that science and exegesis are *human* interpretations of *God's* revelation. Nature must be studied and tested, and Scripture read and re-read, so that we understand them better.

Because there are two texts of revelation, I suggest that Christians look toward Nature and Scripture with a spirit of *equity*. Each text has its voice; we must listen to both.

Rightly balancing the Two Books

The idea behind equity is one of fairness. Fairness does not mean that each text has equal weight or contribution to every issue. Instead, we study each revelation for all that can be gained from it, granting that it has a unique voice and a boundary (or *domain*) of topics to what it can speak.

Earlier, we looked at the theologies revealed by Nature and Scripture. Now we turn from theology to science. What do our studies of the two texts show us about the natural world? What are their domains so that we know what to learn from them? Here are four starting points for those who want to give proper balance to each text.

First, science itself is a dialogue between *multiple* "texts" or sources of data. There is no sole source of information in Nature—there are billions. Astronomers work with light spectra; geologists look at visual and chemical changes in rock. Also, each major conclusion is an accumulation of many pieces of evidence from these sources. Thus scientific conclusions are never merely 'right' or 'wrong.' They are assigned a degree of confidence or a measure of error.

Second, what science reveals to us is fundamentally limited by its methods. Howard Van Till, a physicist and philosopher of science, writes:

> While natural science can fruitfully investigate the *formation* of various structures within the physical world, it is incapable of dealing with the ultimate *origin* of the world's existence. . . .

> While natural science can fruitfully investigate the *behavior* of the physical universe, it is incapable of settling the fundamental questions concerning its *governance*.[12]

Why is science limited in this way? Because it uses natural tools of study. A spectrograph points to the composition of a star; a geologist's hammer to a snapshot of earth history. By using these tools, we are never able to investigate what is super-natural or meta-physical. Science is simply unable to answer every question that we ask.

Third, Scriptural exegesis involves a dialogue between *multiple* texts. The Bible is not one book; it is a collection of many works with different purposes, authors, and editors. Although God is the ultimate author, each human writer lived within a specific cultural setting. As we learned at the start of this essay, the Bible does not address every question we ask. The most certain conclusions we can draw from Scripture are found in Christian statements of faith. But other conclusions, both theological and scientific, we must hold less tightly.

In fact, science occasionally helps us to identify misunderstandings of Scripture. For example, scholars agree Galileo was right to say that the medieval Church misinterpreted astronomy in Psalm 96:10. It is because of science that we affirm the earth is not fixed in space! Theologian R. C. Sproul, a co-author of the *Chicago Statement on Inerrancy*, writes:

> To say that science cannot overturn the teaching of Scripture is not to say that science cannot aid the church in understanding Scripture, or even correct false inferences drawn from Scripture or actual misinterpretations...[13]

Fourthly, what Scripture teaches about the natural world is limited by the authors' intentions. For example, the Bible makes numerous statements that include peripheral natural details: Job 38:29–30 reads, "Who gives birth to the frost from the heavens, when the waters become hard as stone?" Since these words serve the author's main point (that God is Creator) we do not expect them to be scientifically precise. Snow and ice are not as hard as stone. On the other hand, the Bible makes straightforward claims about the origin and governance of the universe: Colossians 1:17 says of Christ that "all things were created through him and for him. He is before all things, and in him all things hold together." As clearly intended by the author, these words answer a central question: *What or who is behind it all?*

In general, I would suggest that the Scripture does not answer most of our detailed questions about Nature. Why? Because the purpose of most biblical passages is theological rather than scientific. If any scientific questions are answered in the Bible, we must first demonstrate that they are the intended concerns of the author. We cannot impose a foreign meaning upon the text. On the other hand, the Bible does claim to be our source of theology (2 Timothy 3:15). So let us remember that the *theological* order of the Two Books matters. We begin with the light of the risen Christ, and we read God's Creation in that light.[14]

Four centuries ago, Galileo proposed that physical experiments are the only way to test whether the sun circles the earth, whereas the Bible is our clear guide to the human situation. I suggest we join him in this approach. Scripture and Nature are both God's vehicles of truth. As we strive for a Christian approach to science, let us study them with a spirit of equity. Our questions about the Two Books are extremely valuable. So onward we go!

~

The heavens declare the glory of God;
the skies proclaim the work of his hands.
Psalm 19:1

For discussion

1. What is something new that you learned in this essay?

2. What are some drawbacks to treating the Two Books of revelation *equally* rather than *equitably*?

3. Augustine wrote, *"The pages of Scripture can only be read by those who know how to read and write, while everyone, even the illiterate, can read the book of the universe."*[15] What are some pitfalls of developing our theology of God solely from Nature without using Scripture as a guide?

4. What are some pitfalls of drawing scientific conclusions solely from Scripture without confirming them through independent physical experiments?

5. Why is it important to know that some Bible passages about Nature are not technically precise? What are some ways to decide which passages are less precise?

6. Do you think Jesus' resurrection is a peripheral statement (i.e., not intended as precise or literal), or is it a primary claim of Scripture? How can we know?

7. Why is it important to assign a degree of confidence or measure of error to conclusions in science?

8. Could we assign a degree of confidence or measure of error to statements in our theology? How so?

9. How much weight do you think Church tradition and scientific consensus should each have in affirming our understandings about nature?

10. What questions do you have after reading this essay?

[1] Church debates on the Trinity, geological history, and human rights began in the 4th, 19th, and 20th centuries, respectively.

[2] See Giuseppe Tanzella-Nitti, "The Two Books Prior to the Scientific Revolution," in *Perspectives on Science and Christian Faith* 57, no. 3 (2005): 237.

[3] See also Acts 17:24–28 and Colossians 1:16.

[4] See also Psalm 119:105 and 2 Peter 1:21.

[5] Old-earth astronomer Hugh Ross attempts to find the scientific method in the Bible, with dubious success. Hugh Ross, *More Than a Theory*, 257.

[6] One source reads: "But let every good and true Christian understand that wherever truth may be found, it belongs to his Master." Saint Augustine, *On Christian Doctrine*, 2.18.

[7] Galileo Galilei, "Letter to the Grand Duchess Christina," quoted in Stillman Drake, *Discoveries and Opinions of Galileo*, 182.

[8] Henry Morris and John Whitcomb, *The Genesis Flood: the Biblical Record and its Scientific Implications*, xxvi–xvii.

[9] Richard Dawkins, *The God Delusion*, 58–59, 61.

[10] Kurt Wise, "Geology," in *In Six Days: Why Fifty Scientists Choose to Believe in Creation*, ed. John Ashton, 355.

[11] Galileo, "Letter to the Grand Duchess," in Drake, 186.

[12] Howard Van Till, et al. *Science Held Hostage: What's Wrong With Creation Science AND Evolutionism*, 20–21.

[13] R. C. Sproul, *Scripture Alone: The Evangelical Doctrine*, 152–153.

[14] See George Murphy, "Reading God's Two Books," in *Perspectives on Science and Christian Faith* 58, no. 1 (2006): 64–67.

[15] Augustine, *Expositions on the Book of Psalms*, 45.7 (Psalm 46 in English bibles), quoted in Tanzella-Nitti, 237. Note that most translations are abridged and do not include this quote. See *Patrologia Latina* 36, 518 for the original Latin text.

4

Curiosity:
embracing the goal of science

Suppose you find a triangular stone in your backyard, embedded in a layer of rock. Once freed from the ground, the object is as large as your hand and has sharp, serrated edges. It appears to be a mineral—and yet it seems strangely lifelike. Soon you find many more. How would you go about deciding where the stone came from?

People in ancient times found such triangular objects throughout the Mediterranean. An early Roman naturalist, Pliny the Elder, thought they had fallen from the heavens, but many scholars suggested that they had spontaneously condensed from fluids within the earth. During the Renaissance the objects were called tongue stones— perhaps the petrified tongues of dragons or snakes—and were used as a remedy for sickness or worn as charms.

It was only in the 17th century that a better explanation was proposed. In 1666, the Danish priest-scientist named

Nicolaus Steno dissected a rare discovery, a beached shark. Upon comparison he found that its teeth were remarkably similar to tongue stones, only smaller, "as one egg resembles another." As you or I might do today, he made a natural conclusion: tongue stones were the preserved teeth of gigantic sharks (Figure 4.1).[1] Steno's paper became even more famous because of the way he extended his thinking to other geological oddities. He concluded that many of the shell-like objects found in the Alps were the remains of oysters, clams, and mussels buried in an ancient seafloor. Steno's influence began a new era in our understanding of fossils and the history of rock layers.[2]

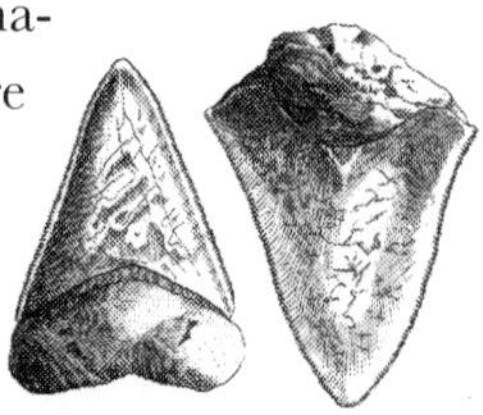

Throughout history, human beings have believed *many* different explanations for what fossils were and where they came from. But surprisingly few ever thought these objects were the dead creatures of an earlier era. So what caused Steno to propose a new

Fig. 4.1

explanation? And how did his idea become the accepted explanation of fossils that we understand today?

In this case, an investigation made all the difference. Steno did what we might call today a *comparative study*. Steno was one of many scientists in the Church who radically deepened our understanding of God's creation by changing their approach to learning. People increasingly recognized that a careful, hands-on interest in the details of nature was fruitful. And over time, it became the process we now know as the scientific method.

Unfortunately, the scientific process is not always understood or used carefully. Some people use faulty science to support a destructive morality or promote an unhealthy medicine. Others oppose well-tested science when, in fact, they do not even understand the details. And what is the result in our society? Damaged confidence in the reliability of science as a whole. Rather than having *curiosity*—a deep inquisitiveness about the details of nature—people develop *skepticism*. Today an increasing number of people wonder what they can trust from science.

Carefulness in science matters. Have you ever heard a skeptical statement about science, one that was (perhaps) a bit light on the details? For example, I once heard someone say, "I heard that a live mollusk was carbon-dated to be 2,300 years old; how come scientists are ignoring this?" I've heard others say, "Doesn't the evidence show that all rock layers were created rapidly by a massive Flood in Genesis?"

These are erroneous statements with researchable, and often easy, answers for the curious.

For example, consider the question of whether rock layers were all formed in the Flood. A few years ago, I backpacked in Glacier National Park, Montana (*photo at right*). The mountains in Glacier are composed almost entirely of sedimentary rocks, which are made of eroded rock fragments from wind, water, or other weathering processes.[3]

My wife and I regularly saw exposures of rock which alter-

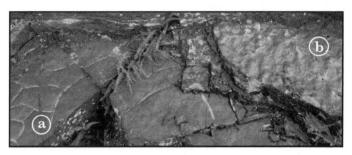

Fig. 4.2 Mud cracks (a) and ripples (b) in Glacier National Park.

nated between layers of dried mud cracks and layers of shallow ripples (Figure 4.2). In fact, we hiked over 30 miles and we saw these layers at every elevation along the way.

Can you imagine hiking through 5,000 vertical feet of pencil-thin layers with alternating signs of water and sun? My words do not do justice to this profound visual experience. After backpacking in Glacier, I began to understand why simple explanations such as "the whole earth was under water for a year" are not taken for granted by geologists, who delight to find an explanation that makes sense of *all* the visible evidence. A scientist at heart is both an explorer and a problem-solver.

In this case, geologists propose that the rock layers in Glacier were formed in shallow seas or lakes that would dry out. This is partly because of the visible ripples and cracks, and partly because fine-grained silt (as is found in the rock) only settles in calm water. The settling rate is a measurable detail in a laboratory; it is proportional to the grain size and the turbulence of the water.[4] So it is not likely that a deluge like Noah's Flood created the mudstone in Glacier National Park. A year-long flood does not allow the time for a half-million layers of silt to individually settle, nor to dry out and crack before being covered again. A more likely possibility is that a fluctuating lake or shallow sea (with rivers as a sediment source) deposited them over time.[5]

We can resolve one level of skepticism about science in this example: geologists are generally very thoughtful about their work. They are not careless, hasty, or ignorant about the details. Many observations have gone into the current explanation about the formation of the rocks in Glacier.

In short, even though most of us are not professional scientists, we still need an eager carefulness in order to form opinions about issues in modern science. When we study nature, the truth will be found in the details.

Getting to know the details

Science is clearly a detail-driven activity. One conse-quence is that when we hear skeptical comments about scientific data, we know we can do some homework. This is especially true in Christian circles when concerns about science are raised. Rather than absorb one another's doubts blindly, our first task is to learn the details of the science—to get as close to the source as we can. That would be a great step for anyone.

But in addressing skepticism toward science, there is a second task in front of us as well. Someone might ask, "Isn't it possible to deceive ourselves and only see what we want to see?" This question is valuable because it reflects a healthy kind of skepticism: wondering if our interpre-tations of the world are reliable. In other words, if nature "speaks for itself," we need to know how to interpret it so that our preconceptions do not mislead us. Therefore the second task is to have a clearer understanding of science itself. We will do this by asking two questions:

I. WHAT IS THE GOAL OF SCIENCE?

In simplest terms, what aim should a scientist have as he or she tries to explain something in nature? Fortunately, that is not a new question. Here are some examples of past scientists who wrote about the goal of science:

(Please refer to primary sources on the next page.)

1) Nicolaus Copernicus, in the 16th century, published his Sun-centered (or *heliocentric*) theory of the solar system because he was driven to find a simpler theory than all others. In the preface to his book, he wrote that he wanted to explain the orbits of the planets in a logically consistent (and beautiful) way without any unnecessary complications. Copernicus pointed out that the earth-centered theory of his day was overly complex and yet failed to predict many details of the planetary orbits.

2) Johannes Kepler, a contemporary of Galileo in the 17th century, believed that God had created a world of pre-dictable, mathematical regularity, not one that was animated by mysterious or divine forces. The goal of his science was to provide the equations that describe how things work. Like many other astronomers and philo-sophers at the dawn of the scientific revolution, Kepler saw the universe as a kind of machine.

3) Louis Agassiz, a natural historian in the 19th century, argued that scientists should search for truth regardless of its usefulness; the purest goal is to explain, not to apply. In his mind, the task of science (specifically

ON THE GOAL OF SCIENCE

Copernicus, *On the Revolutions of the Heavenly Spheres* (1543):

> Your Holiness, I would have you know that what moved me to conceive a different model for explaining the motions of the universal spheres was merely my realization that the astronomers are not consistent among themselves regarding this subject. In the first place, they are so uncertain concerning the motions of the sun and the moon that they can neither observe nor predict even the constant length of a tropical year. Secondly, in calculating the motions of these as well as the other five planets, they do not use the same principles and assumptions, nor the same explanations for their apparent revolutions and motions. . . .

> It began to irritate me that the philosophers, who otherwise scrutinized so precisely the minutiae of this world, could not agree on a more reliable theory concerning the motions of the system of the universe, which the best and most orderly Artist of all framed for our sake. . . . I finally found that if the motion of the other planets is viewed in relation to the circular motion of the earth, and if this calculation is made for the revolution of each planet, then not only do the phenomena follow consistently, but also the orders and magnitudes of all the orbs and spheres and heaven itself are so interconnected that not one of its parts could be removed.[6]

Johannes Kepler, in a letter to Hans Herwart (1605):

> I am much occupied with the investigation of the physical causes. My aim is to show that the heavenly machine is not a kind of divine, live being, but a kind of clockwork (and he who believes that a clock has a soul, attributes the maker's glory to the work), insofar as nearly all the manifold motions are caused by a most simple, magnetic and material force, just as all motions of the clock are caused by a simple weight. I will also show how these physical causes are to be given numerical and geometrical expression.[7]

ON THE GOAL OF SCIENCE   *continued*

Louis Agassiz, in *Methods of Study in Natural History* (1863):

> The community should foster the purely intellectual efforts of scientific men as carefully as they do their elementary schools. . . . For from what other source shall we derive the higher results that are gradually woven into the practical resources of our life, except from the researches of those very men who study science, not for its uses, but for its truth? It is this that gives it its noblest interest: it must be for truth's sake, and not even for the sake of its usefulness to humanity, that the scientific man studies Nature. The application of science to the useful arts requires other abilities, other qualities, other tools than his; and therefore I say that the man of science who follows his studies into their practical application is false to his calling. The practical man stands ever ready to take up the work where the scientific man leaves it, and to adapt it...[8]

Richard Feynman, in "The Pleasure of Finding Things Out," *BBC Horizon* (1981):

> If you expected science to give all the answers to the wonderful questions about what we are, or where we are going, what the meaning of the universe is, and so on, then I think you could easily become disillusioned and then look for some mystic answer to these problems. . . . We are exploring; we're trying to find out as much as we can about the world. People say to me, "Are you looking for the ultimate laws of physics?" No, I'm not. I'm just looking to find out more about the world. And if it turns out there is a simple ultimate law that explains everything, so be it. That would be very nice to discover. If it turns out it's like an onion with millions of layers and we're just sick and tired of looking at the layers, then *that's* the way it is. But whatever way it comes out, its nature is there and she's going to come out the way she *IS*. And therefore, when we go to investigate it, we shouldn't pre-decide what it is that we're trying to do, except to find out more about it.[9]

geology and biology) is simply to put together the clues left behind by the "mind of the Creator." Application is left up to others. Among his many discoveries, Agassiz was the first to suggest that many rock formations in Europe resulted from glaciers moving across the landscape, the evidence of an ancient Ice Age.

4) Richard Feynman, a 20th century physicist who studied subatomic particles, believed that science is a humble exploration of the unknown which focuses on physical explanations for how the world works. Science should not be sidetracked by searching for ultimate or "mystical" meaning. Although he had no interest in religion, Feynman's rapt wonder for nature was still very evident. He once said, "The fact that there are rules at all to be checked is kind of a miracle."[10]

Although they are separated by hundreds of years, these scientists agree on a central goal of science: to find explanations of the world that are both (a) logical and (b) physical. In this way, we have a useful operational boundary. Science is *limited* by the goal to find simple, natural explanations for everything in nature. At the same time, science is *empowered* by this limitation. It allows many different scientists to work together and discover more about the world.

When science is restricted to seeking natural causes, investigators can no longer be satisfied by a simple "God did it" answer to their questions. The tools they use in science—scopes, equations, vials, models—do not even provide that kind of an answer. And this limitation turns out to be very good because it forces a scientist to ask more questions. Take genetics: did you learn about Mendel's pea plants in school? What if his rules of dominant/recessive traits were simply labeled as a God-given quirk of nature? What if the discovery was never followed by a deeper investigative question, such as *What is the carrier of these traits?* We would not have the robust understanding of DNA that we have today.

It is difficult to argue with the enormous fruitfulness of this *How-does-it-work?* approach to science. Over the past four centuries, scientists just like Copernicus, Kepler, Agassiz, and Feynman brought about a scientific revolution by keeping a remarkably simple focus to their work. Humanity can know nature (and in many ways control it) because of this basic curiosity to seek physical explanations for how the world works.

II. Can Science Reveal What Is True About Nature?

The second big question is about the power of the scientific method as our tool of discovery. Can science tell us what is real, true, or factual about the world? Unfortunately, despite the enormous success of science as a whole, today there remains ongoing disagreement about whether science can faithfully interpret what is "out there."

On one extreme is a very skeptical view of knowledge. Consider these words from a popular young-earth apologist, Ken Ham, who regularly participates in creation-evolution debates. He describes his view like this:

> I actually have the same evidence the evolutionist has—the battle is not about the evidence or facts, as they are all the same. We live on the same earth, in the same universe, with the same plants and animals, the same fossils. The facts are all the same . . . Ultimately, the argument is about how you *interpret* the facts—and this depends upon your

belief about history. The real difference is that we have different "histories" (accounts about what happened in the past), which we use to interpret the science and facts of the present.[11]

In other words, according to Ham, the *same* facts or data will point us to *different* conclusions depending on our pre-existing beliefs. Thus, in his view, scientists always need an external guide to correct errors in their work. Ham and other young-earth creationists argue that the Bible is the only proper guide for all sciences (especially for sciences that study the past, such as geology or astronomy).

As it relates to scientific work, the downside to this approach is that we may end up believing that the facts of nature are interpreted equally well from any standpoint— that the answers are determined only by one's prior assumptions. In other words, scientific study *on its own* cannot reveal anything true about nature. And I suggest that this is actually a form of *relativism*.

To use an analogy, in this view science only acts as a mirror to our preconceptions or existing beliefs:

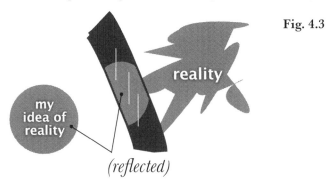

Fig. 4.3

reality

my idea of reality

(reflected)

I believe that this is a rather skeptical view of human knowledge: that the evidence we find in nature cannot speak for itself, somehow or someway. Relativism is a more recent trend in philosophy, but it will lead us to distrust anything in science that conflicts with what we already believe. Relativism is an easy excuse to retreat from the truly God-given task of studying the details.

On the other extreme is an overly positive view of human knowledge. Consider the words of early scientist and philosopher, Sir Francis Bacon:

> If any human being earnestly desire[s] to push on to new discoveries instead of just retaining and using the old; to win victories over Nature as a worker rather than over hostile critics as a disputant; to attain, in fact, clear and demonstrative knowledge instead of attractive and probable theory; [then] we invite him as a true son of Science to join our ranks.[12]

For Bacon, the only thing necessary to enlighten ourselves is to take a look outside and use the scientific method. In this viewpoint, science is a clear window to the real world:

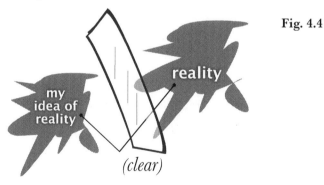

Fig. 4.4

Modern scholars point out that this approach is false as well.[13] Bacon's view is an early form of *positivism*. Positivism is a belief that the facts in nature are *accessible and unambiguous* to anyone who looks. In a sense, Sir Francis Bacon was merely expressing the high optimism of the early scientific revolution. But unfortunately, one's interpretations of nature are *always* filtered, by personality, family, experiences, or religion. The world we live in is complex. Taken too far, positivism sets a precedent of overconfidence and leads us to think that the scientific method provides answers to everything. It is an excuse to ignore the genuine limits of science.

Therefore, how do we learn something meaningful about nature by using a method that (a) relies on practical, natural explanations but (b) leaves the interpretation up to human beings? How can we trust that the scientific method will show us the reality of things?

I suggest we need a new attitude toward investigation. We need a good "middle road" that allows us to walk between skepticism and overconfidence as we do science. This middle road starts with an attitude of *curiosity*.

Curiosity about the details

In short, human discovery is a bit like walking through a dense fog. Common sense tells us that a real world exists outside of ourselves, but we cannot see it clearly. That is the reason why human knowledge moves forward slowly. Our perspectives are both useful and limited. So what do we do? We ask good questions. Not getting the clearest answers at first, we follow up by asking even more questions. This is the true task of science. The attitude of curiosity is marked by a tendency to ask questions.

The technical name for this approach to knowledge is *critical realism*. It strikes a healthy balance between relativism and positivism. It neither relies on preexisting interpretations, nor is it overconfident in its own interpretations.

Critical realism is profoundly useful in science, as well as in philosophy and theology. Theologian and philosopher, N. T. Wright, summarizes it this way:

> [Critical realism] is a way of describing the process of "knowing" that acknowledges the reality of the thing known, as something other than the knower—hence "realism"—while fully acknowledging that the only access we have to this reality lies along the spiraling path of appropriate dialogue or conversation between the knower and the thing known—hence "critical."[14]

Now we can use a new analogy. In this view, science functions like a hazy or dirty window through which we have a partial but steadily-improving view of reality:

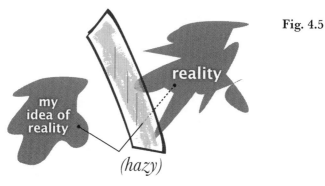

Fig. 4.5

reality

my idea of reality

(hazy)

Critical-realistic science is therefore a process of continual question-asking. On this "middle road," we focus on getting regular *feedback* from the evidence. Specifically, this means testing ideas, evaluating results, and trying again. We also need input from other people who have different interpretations of the evidence. The additional step allows any mistaken beliefs about nature to be challenged.

Can you see how curiosity promotes the discovery of truth in science? Curiosity motivates us to improve on our explanations for the "facts." Without a strong drive to ask questions, this process will stall. But our interest keeps us going, challenging us to refine what we think we know. Because we remain engaged, our ideas about the world will inch closer and closer to the truth.

Moreover, curiosity helps everyone to avoid the trap of unnecessary skepticism. Curiosity is not the opposite of skepticism; it is the antidote. We do not need to trust scientific results blindly. Instead, we need an inquisitive spirit to seek out useful sources for information and perspective. Science requires a shift from deductive learning (looking to external guides) to inductive learning (testing our experiences). But skepticism toward science itself is unnecessary as long as we remain good question-askers.

Earlier, we asked, *Can science reveal what is real and true about nature?* In conclusion, the answer is a resounding *YES!* The scientific method leads us toward real explanations for what we see in nature. The evidence can indeed speak for itself—more so if you are persistent and curious. So if you wonder, "What killed the dinosaurs?" or "Is planet Earth really warming?" the way to discern between the options is to evaluate all of the evidence—in detail—from many different angles. We can have confidence in the process.

This leads us back to the contradiction of the 2,300-year-old living mollusk mentioned earlier. Were scientists ignoring this "fact"? Well, I remember the delight of finding a technical summary about the history of radiocarbon dating. There were a few surprises in it for me. Did you know that one of the first things scientists did after the invention of the technique in 1949 was to test the limits of the method? Soon it became clear that radiocarbon dating

Fig. 4.6   Sketch of a fossil ammonite by Martin Lister, a contemporary of Steno, published in the year 1678.[16]

In non-fossilized form, mollusk shells are composed of carbon in the form of calcium carbonate ($CaCO_3$). Fossils are petrified, however; the carbon has been replaced by hard minerals.

did not work for marine animals. This triggered a landslide of research to figure out why. After all, scientists are rarely put off by the unresolved issues in the field.[15]

For the curious: radioactive carbon (C–14) is a normal occurrence in nature alongside regular carbon (C–12), which is non-radioactive. In fact, they are chemically indistinguishable. The C–14 is created when high-energy particles from the sun collide with molecules in the air, and it is distributed quickly by the wind throughout Earth's atmosphere. As plants process carbon dioxide, both C–14 and C–12 are incorporated into the food chain proportionately. Thus we are all slightly radioactive! However, once living things die and cease to take in food, their parts become less radioactive, year by year, as the existing C–14 in them steadily turns (or *decays*) into regular carbon C–12.

In the case of marine environments, scientists in the 1950s soon discovered that carbon dioxide from our atmosphere mixes into the oceans *very* slowly. Marine organisms (like the ammonite in Figure 4.6) ingest carbon dioxide that has circulated in the ocean for many decades; hence a measurable amount of the carbon–14 has already decayed away. The organism will appear older than it actually is. This is known as the marine reservoir effect.

As a result, radiocarbon dates are not used to calculate the exact ages of marine organisms. Contrary to over-hasty reactions about bad or inaccurate science, the "2,300-year-old living mollusk" actually confirms a known limit of the carbon dating method. Researchers were not afraid of the problem but embraced it as part of the discovery process. And the reward of science is simply that: to learn more.

Discovery through careful investigation is the natural outcome of a Christian theology of nature—that human beings are caretakers, or stewards, on behalf of the Creator. One must *know* the details of Creation to be a good steward. The psalmist once wrote that the works of God are "pondered by all who delight in them" (Psalm 111:2). We begin that journey when we take a deeper look at the methods and results in each area of science.

Let us nurture a spirit of curiosity as we explore our questions about the world. Curiosity at its heart is an expression of confidence in God. Science is empowered to do *its work* because we believe that *God's work* in Creation is intelligible, reliable, and good. And curiosity is natural for our faith. As we trust in God, let us excel in the hands-on work of scientific investigation.

~

Great are the works of the LORD; they
are pondered by all who delight in them.
Psalm 111:2

For discussion

1. What is something new that you learned in this essay?

2. The chapter speaks of unbalanced skepticism. Is there a place for healthy skepticism in science? How so?

3. Is it the responsibility of every Christian to study each scientific question for themselves? What are the alternatives if this is not possible?

4. Should we treat all sources of scientific information with the same value? How do we evaluate between them?

5. How can we go about finding trustworthy voices who think differently than us about science?

6. *"To ask the proper question is half of knowing."*[17] Do you think that this is a fair approach to science? Why or why not?

7. In your mind, what are some characteristics of "faulty" science and "sound" science?

8. Do you think it is possible to do science without bias? What can a scientist do to limit the influence of personal bias in their research?

9. The simple focus of science—seeking physical answers rather than assuming that "God did it"—is often called *methodological naturalism*. This is distinct from the belief that there is no God at all, which is *philosophical naturalism*. How can methodological naturalism help, or limit, our understanding of the world?

10. How comfortable are you with not knowing all the answers to your important questions about science?

[1] Quoted in A. Cutler, *The Seashell on the Mountaintop*, 59. Pictured is Steno's drawing of a tongue stone in *Elemental Specimens of Myology* (1669), 135. Image source: beic.it / BEIC.

[2] See Martin J. S. Rudwick, *Earth's Deep History*, 39–49. Steno's rules of stratigraphy are indispensable to earth science today.

[3] The grains in the mudstone (known as argillite) are slightly metamorphosed and best described as *metasedimentary*.

[4] Stokes Law computes the velocity of a sphere (s) in fluid (f) as $2gR^2(\rho_s-\rho_f)/9\mu$, where ρ is the difference in density, R is the radius, μ is the fluid viscosity, and g is the gravitational constant.

[5] References in David Rockwell, *Exploring Glacier National Park*, 8.

[6] Nicolaus Copernicus, *On the Revolutions of the Heavenly Spheres*, preface.

[7] Johannes Kepler, "Letter to Hans Herwart," quoted in Arthur Koestler, *The Sleepwalkers*, 345.

[8] Louis Agassiz, *Methods of Study in Natural History*, 23–24.

[9] Richard Feynman, "The Pleasure of Finding Things Out," interview for BBC *Horizon*, aired 23 November 1981.

[10] Feynman, *The Meaning of it All: Thoughts of a Citizen Scientist*, ed. Michelle Feynman and Carl Feynman, 43.

[11] Ken Ham, "Searching For the 'Magic Bullet'," *Creation* 25(2): 2.

[12] Francis Bacon, *A New Instrument of Science (Novum Organum)*, preface.

[13] For example, see Michael Polanyi, *Personal Knowledge*, 3 and 214.

[14] N. T. Wright, *The New Testament and the People of God*, 35. See also John Polkinghorne, *Quantum Physics and Theology*, 6.

[15] Sheridan Bowman, *Radiocarbon Dating*, 25. See also M. L. Keith and G. M. Anderson, "Radiocarbon Dating: Fictitious Results with Mollusk Shells," *Science* 16 August 1963, 634 637.

[16] Pictured is an ammonite in Lister, *History of the Creatures of England*, 205. Image source: lhldigital.lindahall.org / Linda Hall Library.

[17] Commonly attributed to Roger Bacon, 13th century.

5

Reverence:
loving the world of Scripture

Consider the English language for a moment. Suppose you are able to write a letter to someone who lives in your home town 400 years from now. Naturally, it will be full of phrases common to our culture today. What challenges do you think they will have when they read your words? And what kind of questions will they ask?

Perhaps the easiest way to appreciate such questions is to look to our own past and attempt to read a play by Shakespeare. Who among us has not grappled with understanding older English? We do understand Shakespeare, of course, but most of us read his words slowly because of their unfamiliar style and rhythm. Just as importantly, we also need a guide to the idioms, references, and even science of 17th century England.[1] The plain meaning of Shakespeare's words are not always clear to us. I believe the challenge is no different for our modern English.

For example, these phrases are generally understandable to anyone, but their real power is lost unless we know their point of reference:

"Houston, we've had a problem." 1970
"One does not simply walk into Mordor." 2001

Here are some phrases that are loaded with sharp irony, but only if you know the original story:

"Go ahead, make my day." 1983
"May the odds be ever in your favor." 2012

The phrases below are unclear unless you are well-versed in popular media:

"May be the Force be with you." 1977
"Drop the mic." 1983

And these phrases have such a well-known and unspoken context that they can be used as an inside joke anywhere:

"My precioussssss."
"Guenther. *Dan* Guenther." (insert your name here)

I suspect that someone who reads today's language in the future will think that our English is quite alien—as much as Shakespeare is to us. Why? Because the words, phrases, and idioms in every language shift over time. The reader needs to know the original context or else he or she will be lost. And what about broader forms of speech, such as satire? Satires do not typically announce their genre. A future reader will completely miss the subtle edge of the dialogue unless they understand its points of reference.

Likewise, the Bible is a collection of writings that are alien to our modern ears. The authors lived in a Hebrew culture very different than ours. And they were not *simply*

Hebrew. They also debated Roman politics, quoted Greek philosophers, and wrote to people who were immersed in Mesopotamian, Egyptian, and Canaanite religions. If we are to follow Scripture as God's word, then we must have a deep respect and even *reverence* for how its human authors recorded God's revelation within a very ancient context.

Knowing the context helps us to solve interpretation problems in the New Testament. For example, have you heard an accusation that Apostle Paul supported slavery? Some quote Paul's instruction, "Slaves, obey your earthly masters" (Colossians 3:22). But knowing that the Romans crushed any challenge to the social order, Paul's advice was actually quite shrewd in context. Here is the second part of his command: "…to curry favor, but with sincerity of heart and reverence for the Lord." So Paul encouraged Roman slaves to subvert their situation by practicing Christ-like devotion. Human equality is quite evident in his letters, which is why 18th century slavery abolitionists freely quoted Paul for their cause—"There is no Greek or Jew, circumcised or uncircumcised, barbarian, Scythian, slave or free, but Christ is all" (Colossians 3:11).[2] New Testament interpretation begins with understanding its Roman context.

And how about the Old Testament world? Have you ever studied the first chapters of Genesis in light of their context? The Hebrews who received these words were themselves a *product* of other cultures in the ancient Near East. Their forebears carried idols in Mesopotamia, lived for centuries in Egypt, and often reverted to worshipping nature gods in Canaan.[3] Thus we should expect to find cultural references in Genesis which make sense only to an ancient Near Eastern audience.

Cultural references are especially helpful guides when it comes to answering scientific questions in the Bible. For example, why do you suppose the sun and moon in Genesis 1:14–16 are described only as "great lights"?

> And God said, "Let there be lights in the expanse of the sky to separate the day from the night, and let them serve as signs to mark seasons and days and years, and let them be lights in the expanse of the sky to give light on the earth." And it was so. God made two great lights—the greater light to govern the day and the lesser light to govern the night. He also made the stars.

The Hebrew words for "sun" and "moon" are *shemesh* and *yareach*. And yet they are never used in the Creation account of Genesis. Why? Perhaps you would be interested to hear that *shemesh* and *yareach* have the same verbal roots as ancient Near Eastern deities, since Israel's language developed from the cultures around it. Shamash is the Babylonian sun god; Yarich is the Canaanite moon god.[4] As illustrated in Figure 5.1, nature gods dominated nearby cultures. So it seems that the biblical author avoided any reference to other deities in the Creation account. And this is not the only example. We also see in verse 2 that God's spirit hovers *above* a passive ocean—a chaos deity in Mesopotamia, and the pantheon of stars receive only a casual mention in verse 16 ("He also made the stars").

Therefore, a not-so-subtle intention in Genesis 1 is to dethrone the many nature gods in the minds of God's chosen people. The Hebrews struggled to separate from their polytheistic neighbors. Recall the first commandment, "You shall have no other gods before me" (Exodus 20:3), or Moses' challenge to Israel: "When you look up to the sky

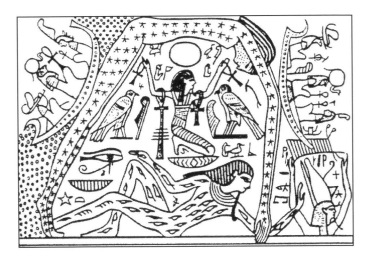

Fig. 5.1 Drawing from an Egyptian tomb depicting the cosmos. The goddess of sky, Nut, arches overhead and is embedded with stars. Shu, the god of air, supports her. The sun god Ra sails in the heavenly waters above, and earth god Geb reclines below. Similar pantheons are found in Canaan and Mesopotamia.[5]

and see the sun, the moon and the stars . . . do not be enticed into bowing down to them" (Deuteronomy 4:19). The clear message heard by the Hebrews in Genesis 1 was not *when* God made the sun, moon, and stars, but *which* god—the One God who is truly separate from the natural world. In short, just as with the rest of the Bible, interpreting Genesis begins with understanding its ancient world.

Of course, Christians today find themselves more and more distant from that original audience. The world of Israel was covered (quite literally) by the sand of 2,500 years of history. An astonishing number of empires ruled over their land, imposing different ways of life: Babylonian,

Assyrian, Persian, Greek, Roman, Arab, *and* British empires. Archaeologists have uncovered much about Israel's ancient neighbors and their ways of thinking in the last century and half. But this knowledge is so recent that many older Bible commentaries do not even mention the ancient Near Eastern setting of Genesis!

The good news is that these newer discoveries do not change essential Christian theology. Genesis 1 still teaches that God is the sole Creator, regardless of what we know about its nature deity references. Regrettably, our lack of cultural awareness *does* affect what we think the Bible says on the topic of science. Contemporary readers like you and I have quite a challenge. What seems like the "plain meaning" is not always the case.

Whose context is it?

Here is what I am suggesting: that our understanding of the Bible depends on our grasp of its culture. We need proper context in order to know the "plain meaning" of the text, especially as it relates to science. So this leads me to ask: Does the Bible teach about science? In other words, does it teach any practical truths about nature or natural history? And if so, how do we know what it teaches?

Christians over the centuries have held many interesting viewpoints on this question. Here are some examples of past viewpoints on scientific teaching in the Bible:

(Please refer to primary sources on the next page.)

1) Saint Augustine, in the 4th century, argued that the author of Genesis—traditionally, Moses—knew more about astronomy than he revealed to the Israelites. In Genesis 1:6 the earth is covered above by a heavenly disk:

ON SCIENCE IN THE BIBLE

Saint Augustine, in *The Literal Meaning of Genesis* (c. 415):

> It is also frequently asked what our belief must be about the form and shape of heaven according to Sacred Scripture. Many scholars engage in lengthy discussions on these matters, but the sacred writers with their deeper wisdom have omitted them. Such subjects are of no profit for those who seek beatitude, and, what is worse, they take up very precious time that ought to be given to what is spiritually beneficial. What concern is it of mine whether heaven is like a sphere and the earth is enclosed by it and suspended in the middle of the universe, or whether heaven like a disk above the earth covers it over on one side? But the credibility of Scripture is at stake . . . Hence, I must say briefly that in the matter of the shape of heaven the sacred writers knew the truth, but that the Spirit of God, who spoke through them, did not wish to teach men these facts that would be of no avail for their salvation.[6]

John Calvin, in *Commentaries on the First Book of Moses* (1554):

On Genesis 1:16, "He also made the stars":

Moses does not here subtly descant [i.e., carefully teach], as a philosopher, on the secrets of nature, as may be seen in these words. First, he assigns a place in the expanse of heaven to the planets and stars; but astronomers make a distinction of spheres and, at the same time, teach that the fixed stars have their proper place in the firmament. Moses makes two great luminaries; but astronomers prove by conclusive reasons that the star of Saturn, which on account of its great distance appears the least of all, is greater than the moon. Here lies the difference; Moses wrote in a popular style things which, without instruction, all ordinary persons endued with common sense are able to understand; but astronomers investigate with great labor whatever the sagacity of the human mind can comprehend.[7]

ON SCIENCE IN THE BIBLE   *continued*

Jason Lisle, "The Expansion of the Universe," in *The New Answers Book 2* (2008):

> Isaiah 40:22 teaches that God stretches out the heavens like a curtain and spreads them out like a tent to dwell in. This would suggest that the universe has actually increased in size since its creation. God is stretching it out, causing it to expand. Now, this verse must have seemed very strange when it was first written. The universe certainly doesn't look as if it is expanding. After all, if you look at the night sky tonight, it will appear about the same size as it did the previous night, and the night before that. . . . So it must have been tempting for [early] Christians to reject what the Bible teaches about the expansion of the universe. I wonder if any Christians tried to 'reinterpret' Isaiah 40:22 to read it in an unnatural way so that they wouldn't have to believe in an expanding universe. When the secular world believes one thing and the Bible teaches another, it is always tempting to think that God got the details wrong. But God is never wrong.[8]

John Walton, in *The Lost World of Genesis One* (2010):

> Our first proposition is that Genesis 1 is ancient cosmology. That is, it does not attempt to describe cosmology in modern terms or address modern questions. The Israelites received no revelation to update or modify their "scientific" understanding of the cosmos. They did not know that the stars were suns; they did not know that the earth was spherical and moving through space; they did not know that the sun was much further away than the moon, or even further than the birds flying in the air. They believed that the sky was material (not vaporous), solid enough to support the residence of deity as well as to hold back waters. In these ways, and many others, they thought about the cosmos in much the same way that anyone in the ancient world thought, and not at all like anyone thinks today. And God did not think it important to revise their thinking.[9]

the *expanse, vault,* or *firmament* in most English translations. Commenting on this passage, Augustine suggested
that God taught Moses proper astronomy (so that he was
not misled), but inspired Moses to write Genesis using
local beliefs about astronomy so as to not distract from
the essential teaching of salvation.

2) John Calvin, a theologian of the 16th century Protestant
Reformation, suggested that Moses wrote in a non-
scientific manner for an uneducated audience. Moses
referred to some basic facts about astronomy, but did so
within the limits of the Israelites' uneducated background. Like Augustine, Calvin also speculated that God
privately revealed fuller scientific truths to Moses.

3) Jason Lisle, a young-earth astronomer, believes that God
taught the biblical audience about modern astronomy.
Although the expansion of the universe was only demonstrated in 1929, God revealed this truth long ago in
Isaiah 40:22 ("He stretches out the heavens like a tent").
Lisle argues that the early Christians were faced with a
choice: to doubt God's Word, even if modern astronomy made no sense to them, or to believe it at face value.

4) John Walton, an Old Testament theologian, believes God
did not aim to change the audience's existing beliefs
about the physical world. God inspired the Creation
account to carry his intended message. He did this by
using the "world picture"—or physical layout of the
universe—that was held by Israel and its neighbors in
the ancient Near East. Whether directly or indirectly,
the intention of Genesis 1 is not to teach science at all.

These four viewpoints illustrate the important questions that Christians may ask about Bible passages which deal with nature. For example: *Who is 'in the know' about the full scientific truth: God, the author, or both?* or *How much is God concerned to change the existing scientific knowledge of the audience?* or *What is the intended message of the verse or passage?* Asking these questions will help the reader determine whether a verse is making scientific statements.

One way to bring these questions together is to think in terms of a model. Consider two popular approaches for describing the relationship of science to the Bible:

THE BIBLE CONFIRMS MODERN SCIENCE. In other words, God revealed things to the biblical audience—well in advance of their time—which match what we know according to modern (i.e., mainstream) science. Modern science and the Bible say the same thing about nature. This view is called *concordism*. Thus we can use scientific discoveries to understand and confirm various passages in the Bible:

Scripture   Science

Fig. 5.2

shared context: science as a guide

In this model, modern science functions as our guide to the Scripture. One example is Lisle's view of Isaiah 40, in which he believes that God taught the universe is expanding. This is an idea that was only confirmed in the 20th century. Similarly, others believe that the days of Genesis 1 match up scientifically with modern cosmology: "Let there be light" refers to the Big Bang, and so on. Astronomer Hugh Ross once saw scientific details in Genesis as evidence for God:

> The quantity and detail of scientific content far exceeded what I found in the other books. To my surprise, the scientific method was as clearly evident in Genesis 1 as it is in modern research. . . . Only one conclusion made sense to me, the conclusion that the Creator of the universe had something to do with the words of Genesis 1.[10]

THE BIBLE CORRECTS MODERN SCIENCE. In other words, God's revelation in Scripture gives us a scientific under-standing of many aspects of nature. There are many verses which speak plainly to all people on topics of science and natural history. This view is a strong form of *literalism.* Therefore we can use Bible verses to correct mistakes in mainstream science:

Scripture   Science

Fig. 5.3

shared context: the Bible as a guide

In this second model, the Bible is a reliable guide to nature—an "answer key" for science. For example, if God created the universe "in six days" (Genesis 2:2 and Exodus 20:11), then the Big Bang theory is clearly wrong. Likewise, scientists must be in error to think that dinosaurs lived 65 million years ago. Henry Morris, one of the fathers of the Creation Science movement in the 20th century, wrote:

> If one starts with the presupposition that God has written the Bible as His own perfect revelation of the origin, purpose, and destiny of the world, then it again is perfectly possible to correlate all the physical data of science and history within that framework.[11]

In comparing these viewpoints, you might notice that literalism and concordism are really just two sides of the same coin. How so? Both of them make the argument that the Bible teaches science. But where the concordist accepts most mainstream science and looks for similar conclusions in the Bible, the literalist starts with a literal view of the Bible and then relies on an alternative, "creation" science, in order to find similar conclusions in nature.

At the very least, I think these viewpoints demonstrate that confusion exists among Christians about the audience of Scripture. For example, a concordist interprets the Bible as if he or she is the primary audience. In other words, they are the ones *fully in the know* about its meaning. This implies that the original audience did not appreciate—and could not apply—many biblical statements about nature.

On the flip side, a literalist assumes that the scripture speaks plainly to anyone, regardless of culture. They are *equally in the know* as the original audience. And this implies that modern people can point out scientific statements in the Bible without their own presuppositions getting in the way. But of course, 21st century biases *always* get in the way.

Just as we saw earlier, a plain interpretation of the phrase, "God made two great lights," tells modern readers nothing about its surprising significance to the Hebrews.

In the end, what we see here is a lack of appreciation for the context of the ancient audience. Perhaps people are easily fixated on the wrong context—the practical settings of our modern world. And too often, the default ways of reading the Bible lead us away from its intended message. This is especially true for passages about nature. In my estimation, good biblical interpreters must find a balance between the two audiences, old and new.

This balance toward biblical context is best described as an attitude of *reverence*.

Mutual reverence

The attitude of reverence is marked by a high regard for the divine Author and the human agents of Scripture. Reading the Old Testament in its ancient Near Eastern context is a reverent act. Knowing the broader context helps us to distinguish between God's timeless words and their cultural clothing. If believers today do not make this distinction, then we will interpret God's words based on our *own* culture and we will ignore his original audience and message—an irreverent act.

Moreover, biblical reverence draws us into a relationship of mutual honor. First of all, God is honoring toward his audience. God inspired prophets and apostles to write in a way that his people would understand. And secondly, we are also honoring. We accept that the Scripture was given first to other people. When we acknowledge the culture of those who received the Word, we honor God himself.

As a result, the attitude of *reverence* allows us a new way to think about scientific statements in the Bible:

THE BIBLE CONTAINS ANCIENT "SCIENCE". In other words, biblical authors refer to nature in a culturally normal way as they convey the inspired message of God. This view is sometimes called *accommodation.* Therefore we must learn how the Hebrews understood the natural world—their version of science, so to speak. We can interpret the Bible by studying its ancient context and do not assume that it contains modern science:

Scripture   Science

Fig. 5.4

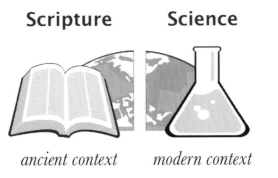

ancient context   *modern context*

Both Augustine and Calvin—theologians separated by a thousand years—argue that God speaks in this way out of necessity. God's primary revelation is about human history, morality, and the plan of redemption. Unfamiliar scientific concepts would have confused or obscured that message. Therefore God "accommodated" himself to his children, speaking his message within Israel's existing knowledge about the world. Calvin wrote:

> For who is so devoid of intellect as not to understand that God, in so speaking, lisps with us as nurses are wont [i.e., accustomed] to do with little children? Such modes of expression, therefore, do not so much express what kind of a

being God is, as accommodate the knowledge of him to our feebleness.[12]

Of course, as we read earlier, Augustine and Calvin also suggested that God gave Moses deeper scientific knowledge. They did not want God to appear to be lying. But I do not think this assumption is helpful or even necessary (i.e., if Moses was privately told the earth is a globe, but then told not to write it down, what purpose could it really serve?).

The main point is this: God speaks our language. That is why Walton's view, quoted earlier, is a great place to begin. Biblical references to natural things should make sense in light of the education of the Hebrew audience—which was a pre-modern view of nature. I think this is a prudent viewpoint which helps us to read the Bible more accurately and sensibly.[13]

As a good example of accommodation, have you ever wondered what the old King James translation means by the word *firmament* in Genesis 1:7?

> And God made the firmament, and divided the waters which were under the firmament from the waters which were above the firmament: and it was so.

Many of our modern translations use the word *expanse*, by which we might think of the Earth's atmosphere. But the old English word *firmament* (Latin *firmamente*) is more true to the meaning since the Hebrew word, *raqia'*, indicates a hard surface. Its verb form, *raqa*, means to stamp or spread out—the image of a blacksmith hammering metal into a sheet. The standard Hebrew lexicon states that the firmament was "regarded by Hebrews as solid, and supporting 'waters' above it."[14] And many Christian theologians in the past held that *raqia'* refers to a dome above the earth.

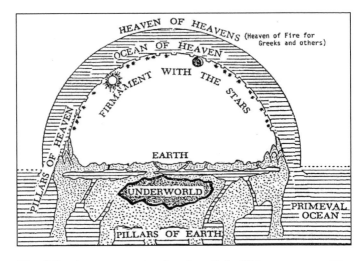

Fig. 5.5   A representative drawing of the Hebrew cosmos. The "waters above" are held up by a firmament or heavenly dome. The sun, moon, and stars are in the firmament. The underworld of *sheol* sits below the earth, alongside the "waters below."[15]

The simplest explanation is that the words in Genesis 1:7 are an ancient perspective of the heavens. Figure 5.5 illustrates this Hebrew world picture, drawn from many descriptions scattered throughout the Old Testament.[16] You can see it is very similar to the Egyptian world picture in Figure 5.1—water sits above the starry firmament with a flat earth below—but the Hebrew picture ignores the nature deities. Clearly this was a normal way to think about the heavens in 2,000 B.C. Therefore Genesis 1:7 accommodates an ancient perspective, but by leaving out the nature deities the creation story teaches a very different theology about God, as Creator and Sustainer. This was a powerful message to any Hebrew coming out of Egypt.

In summary, we make sense of the whole Bible when we hold an attitude of reverence. The primary skill is to ask if a passage teaches *directly* about natural history or processes. In which case the words are not cultural "clothing" at all, but are intended for us to learn. For example, the disciples clearly believed that Jesus was raised physically from the dead, and the apostle Paul is strikingly clear about Jesus' resurrection in 1 Corinthians 15:17. Intentionality is the key to understanding what is written in the Bible. Therefore, when a statement about nature is not the author's primary aim, we should see it as a normal cultural reference. We are always trying to discover and follow the message of God— nothing more and nothing less.

The theologian J. I. Packer, who co-authored *The Chicago Statement on Inerrancy*, writes:

> Scripture is inerrant, not in the sense of being absolutely precise by modern standards, but in the sense of making good its claims and achieving that measure of focused truth at which its authors aimed.[17]

The heart of biblical inspiration is that the Scripture communicates faithfully about God and the human race. Just as God took up limited human form in Jesus, so he expresses himself in ways that his people understand. Revering the God of Scripture means that we also honor the people of Scripture and their world. May it be so!

How precious to me are your thoughts, God!
How vast is the sum of them!
Psalm 139:17

For discussion

1. What is something new that you learned in this essay?

2. How familiar are you with the ancient cultures of Israel and its neighbors in the Old Testament?

3. When we read the Bible but miss some of its cultural references, what do you think we lose in the process?

4. Do you think it is an irreverent act to interpret a Bible passage from the context of our modern culture?

5. When a Bible verse uses an ancient view about nature (for example, when Jesus says that a mustard seed is the smallest of all seeds), do you think that God is affirming false ideas about the universe? Why or why not?

6. Genre plays a large role in how we interpret Scripture. What are some of the markers we can use to know the genre of a passage or story?

7. Isaiah 40:22 reads, *"He stretches out the heavens like a canopy, and spreads them out like a tent to live in."* What do you think "stretches out the heavens" means in this verse? How does the broader passage influence its meaning?

8. "What is the timeless principle?" is a common method for applying the Scripture to modern life. Do you think this is a fair Christian approach to interpretation?

9. What are some possible indicators that we should take a statement in the Bible as a scientific statement?

10. What questions do you have about the relationship between science and Scripture?

[1] For example, see Carla Mazzio, "Shakespeare and Science, c. 1600," *South Central Review* 26, no. 1 (2009): 1–23.

[2] Quoted on the title page of William Wilberforce, *A Letter on the Abolition of the Slave Trade* (1807).

[3] See Genesis 31:19, 35:2; Exodus 3:13, 32:4; and Numbers 25:2.

[4] Bill Arnold and Brent Strawn, *The World Around the Old Testament: The People and Places of the Ancient Near East*, 152.

[5] Image source: E. A. Wallis Budge, "The God Seb supporting Nut on Heaven," in *The Gods of the Egyptians*, vol. 2, facing 95.

[6] Saint Augustine, *The Literal Meaning of Genesis*, 2.9.20.

[7] Calvin, John. *Commentaries on the First Book of Moses*, 1:16.

[8] Jason Lisle, "The Expanding Universe," in *The New Answers Book 2*, ed. Ken Ham, 48–49.

[9] John Walton, *The Lost World of Genesis One*, 14.

[10] Hugh Ross, *The Genesis Question*, 9.

[11] Henry Morris, "The Bible is a Textbook of Science," *Biblioteca Sacra* 121 (Fall 1964): 343.

[12] Calvin, *Institutes of the Christian Religion*, 1.13.1. See also Augustine, *The Literal Meaning of Genesis*, 2.6.13.

[13] See Dan Guenther, "The Accommodation Doctrine," Regent College (June 2010), 14, at academia.edu/33151691.

[14] Brown, Driver, and Briggs, *Hebrew and English Lexicon*, 956. John Walton affirms this point but suggests a different Hebrew word refers to the solid sky; see Barrett, *The Historical Adam*, 68.

[15] Image source: Claus Schedl, "The World Picture of the Creation Account," in *The Ancient Orient and Ancient Biblical History*, 233.

[16] For example, see Genesis 1:6–7, 7:11; 2 Samuel 22:6; 2 Kings 7:2; Psalm 104:2–5, 148:4; Ecclesiastes 1:5; and Isaiah 40:22.

[17] From the Exposition of "The Chicago Statement on Biblical Inerrancy" (1978), in J. I. Packer, *God Has Spoken*, 147.

6

Focus:
maximizing confidence in science

Imagine you have an opportunity to work as a scientist for a season. You can choose a field of study that fascinates you most. Clearing up riddles in the climate, our DNA, the planets—you name it, and you get to do it. The knowledge and working skills will be downloaded into your brain (video game style), and off you go. What kind of work would you want to do?

I have often dreamed about this myself. Before my life took its current direction, I spent my college years in physics labs. My summer jobs at the Pacific Northwest National Laboratory were nothing short of amazing. These days I often dream about paleosciences, since questions about the past dominate many Christian discussions. For example, think about the Ice Age and the early human migrations that followed. The creatures of that time are so strange, fascinating, and yet familiar: saber-toothed tigers, gigantic armadillos, dire wolves, and mastodons as tall as a school bus. Surprisingly, their bones, hides, and hair can still be pulled from tar pits in California and chiseled out of the permafrost in Alaska. I often wonder what it would be like to uncover something new in that prehistoric world.

Unfortunately for thrill seekers, the big "wow" factor of scientific discovery comes with a few reality checks. First of all, the daily grind of research is not very exciting, whether in physics or in paleoscience. Edwin Hubble (for whom the space telescope was named) showed the world in 1929 that the universe is expanding—but he spent an *entire decade* looking at galaxies to show it. And climate scientists live for months in tiny huts on the Greenland ice sheet, pulling ice cores out of mile-deep shafts. Science consists of many repetitive tasks with only a few moments of inspiration.

Secondly, each area of science has a minimum base of knowledge, history, and technical skills that a scientist must master before he or she is effective. No one can learn all of these things overnight. Have you ever heard the expression that it takes 10,000 hours to become an expert in a subject? Whether or not the number is accurate, the point is that it takes a very long time to learn a discipline. There is no easy download (to my dismay).

Most importantly, scientists face a surprising number of uncertainties. Theories are often incomplete in some way and do not answer every question. The data is sometimes ambiguous. And our methods of research are imperfect; techniques often need improvement. So I choose the word *uncertainties* to describe all of the challenges above. A good scientist faces many uncertainties, and she or he needs a strong sense of humility as a result.

The reality that science is difficult is nothing new. Even some Church fathers occasionally mocked the irregularity of early attempts at natural philosophy and science. In the 4th century, Saint Basil wrote:

> The Greeks wrote many works about nature, but not one account among them remained unaltered and firmly established, for the later account always overthrew the preceding one. As a consequence, there is no need for us to refute their words; they avail mutually for their own undoing.[1]

So here lies the challenge: How can we learn anything about nature when we face so many uncertainties in science? This question is clearly one we all need to understand.

Thankfully, efforts at natural science are more fruitful today than they were in the past. Why? Because we have discovered helpful ways to deal with uncertainty. A biblical theology of Creation led early scientists and theologians to believe that nature is predictable and open to the senses. The development of modern scientific methods—the rules of science, so to speak—is a consequence of this belief in an orderly universe. And over the past 500 years, people found ways to *focus* their study of nature and maximize the level of confidence we have in the results.

For example, here are some past scholars writing about the core values in a scientific theory:

(Please refer to primary sources on the next page.)

1) James Hutton, one of the first geologists in the 18th century, thought that a theory should not assume anything about the history of the world. In his time, all rock layers were assumed to be caused by a single large flood

(usually understood to be Noah's Flood). In studying the coastline in Scotland, however, Hutton found rock layers that rested against one another at very extreme angles. He realized the layers could not have formed simultaneously, but came from *different* geological events.

2) C. S. Lewis, in the 20th century, wrote that a good theory should attempt to explain *all* the details or "phenomena" of the subject in the simplest way possible. As a scholar of Medieval literature, he was well-versed in the medieval theory of the universe. Lewis admired the great "Model" with its concentric spheres and hierarchy of creatures, not because of its truth—it was defunct by the 1600s—but because medieval sages tried to "save" and account for every detail of nature in their theory.

3) Karl Popper, in the 20th century, argued that a theory can never be proven beyond doubt and must be exposed to ongoing testing in the real world. This is Popper's famous criteria: a good theory must be falsifiable. It should be possible to prove the theory wrong, or it is not scientific at all. Of course, this means that no theory is ever fully verified, either. Therefore, in actual practice, better theories simply have stronger evidence.

4) Howard Van Till, a retired physicist at Calvin College, writes that a scientific theory must be logically coherent. It cannot have internal contradictions, in which parts of the theory disagree with each other. A good theory should also be applicable everywhere in the universe, not just in one location or one period of time. In other words, we should prefer scientific theories that attempt to describe universal laws.

ON SCIENTIFIC THEORIES

James Hutton, in *A Theory of the Earth* (1788):

> In examining things which actually exist, and which have proceeded in a certain order, it is natural to look for that which had been first; man desires to know what had been the beginning of those things which now appear. But when, in forming a theory of the earth, a geologist shall indulge his fancy in framing without evidence that which had preceded the present order of things, he then either misleads himself, or writes a fable for the amusement of his reader. A theory of the earth, which has for [its] object truth, can have no [assumption about] that which had preceded the present order of this world; for, this order alone is what we have to reason upon; and to reason without data is nothing but delusion.[2]

C. S. Lewis, in *The Discarded Image* (1964):

> A scientific theory must 'save' or 'preserve' the appearances, the phenomena, it deals with, in the sense of getting them all in, doing justice to them. Thus, for example, your phenomena are luminous points in the night sky which exhibit such and such movements in relation to one another and in relation to an observer at a particular point . . . on the surface of the earth. Your astronomical theory will be a supposal such that, if it were true, the apparent [i.e., predicted] motions would be those you actually observed. The theory will then have 'got in' or 'saved' the appearances.

> But if we demanded no more than that from a theory, science would be impossible, for a lively inventive faculty could devise a good many different supposals which would equally save the phenomena. We have therefore had to supplement by another canon — first, perhaps, formulated with full clarity by Occam. According to this second canon we must accept (provisionally) not any theory which saves the phenomena but that theory which does so with the fewest possible assumptions.[3]

ON SCIENTIFIC THEORIES   *continued*

Karl Popper, in *The Logic of Scientific Discovery* (1959):

> Not the **verifiability** but the *falsifiability* of a system is to be taken as a criterion of demarcation. In other words: I shall not require of a scientific system that it shall be capable of being singled out [i.e., proven], once and for all, in a positive sense; but I shall require that its logical form shall be such that it can be singled out, by means of empirical tests, in a negative sense: it must be possible for an empirical scientific system to be refuted by experience. (Thus the statement, 'It will rain or not rain here tomorrow' will not be regarded as empirical, simply because it cannot be refuted; whereas the statement, 'It will rain here tomorrow' will be regarded as empirical.)[4]

Howard Van Till, in *Science Held Hostage* (1988):

> It is perhaps self-evident that an adequate scientific theory should be internally coherent, that it should contain no elements that are logically inconsistent with other elements. We assume that the behavior of physical systems is rationally intelligible, and consequently we expect that our theoretical models for their behavior will be devoid of any internal contradictions.

> But the criterion of coherence has an even broader scope. We expect that not only will the behavior of a particular system or category of systems be internally coherent, but also that the physical behavior of the entire empirically accessible universe will be rationally coherent. Patterns of physical behavior are presumed to be universally applicable—the same patterns in all places and at all times and for all relevant systems.

> The law of energy conservation, for instance, applies not only here on earth, but within the Andromeda Galaxy as well; not only today but three billion years ago in the quasar 3C273 as well; not only for falling apples, but for nuclear reactions as well.[5]

Together, these examples illustrate a focused scientific process. A good theory must: (a) have few assumptions, (b) explain many details simply, (c) be testable and open to review, and (d) make sense inside and out. For example, the claim, *Iron oxide makes Mars red*, will be more useful than the claim, *The Roman god of war made Mars red*. It is testable and can be used to explain more about the world. Moreover, the core values of a good theory go hand in glove with the scientific method: the focused cycle of hypothesis, testing, and revision we use to verify theories. Thus, all of modern science is built on the posture or discipline of *focus*—using theories and methods that have a narrow, limited scope.

This essay aims to help the average person be more confident with a focused scientific process. Most of us probably feel that we lack expertise when scientific debates heat up around us. The discipline of focus helps us know what to do. (Plus, it is a better option than trying to decide between loud opinions in the media!)

To this end, I have chosen a case study so that we can model focused question-asking. Our topic is a recent area of climate research: ice cores in Greenland. Then we will look at some important aspects of scientific theories.

Case study on *focus*: Greenland ice cores

From 1989 to 1993, climate researchers extracted a core nearly two miles long from the ice sheet in Greenland. The *Greenland Ice Sheet Project 2*, or GISP2, took five years and produced a frozen vertical record of snowfall and atmospheric conditions in the northern hemisphere. The team of scientists published a count of layers of snow that goes back 110,000 years. You may wonder: How is it possible to count so many layers in an ice core? Here is a brief look.

In short, as snow falls on top of the ice sheet, things such as dust particles, air bubbles, and atmospheric acids are trapped between the snow crystals. These "markers" remain as the snow is compacted and slowly becomes ice. The markers also vary noticeably between seasons, providing a distinction between each annual layer of snowfall. The ice layers are also visible to the naked eye and can be counted by hand. Teams of scientists work together on ice cores, often documenting their progress on blogs.[6]

The GISP2 ice core is a remarkable feat of engineering (imagine a narrow tube extending 3,015 meters down to bedrock!). And it has proven even more remarkable for our study of the climate. Using the GISP2 and other nearby cores, we have made tremendous strides in our understanding of past climates—for example, the "Little Ice Age" from 1550–1850 A.D. in which plunging temperatures led to long winters, short growing seasons, and famine.

Naturally, many uncertainties complicate the study of ice cores. Over the years, I have read through a dozen or so major papers by the researchers who analyze the GISP2. Addressing uncertainties in order to draw better conclusions is a major goal of this technical writing. The GISP2 teams (led by scientists Richard Alley, Debra Meese, and others) published numerous papers on their methods. However, the uncertainties also open an opportunity for critics to doubt the reliability of ice core science. These criticisms come mainly from some advocates of young-earth creationism, who find it very difficult to accept the idea of 110,000 annual layers (i.e., years) in an ice core.

It is impossible here to describe every criticism raised.

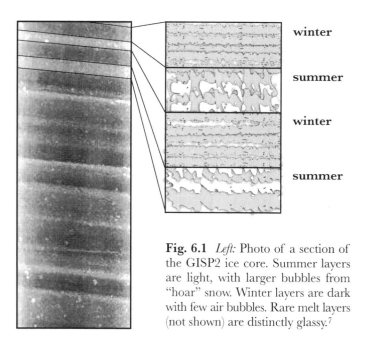

Fig. 6.1 *Left:* Photo of a section of the GISP2 ice core. Summer layers are light, with larger bubbles from "hoar" snow. Winter layers are dark with few air bubbles. Rare melt layers (not shown) are distinctly glassy.[7]

But my synopsis is that those criticisms center on two main issues: (1) whether the dust, air, and acid markers are a good indicator of annual snow layers; and (2) whether the scientists who interpret ice cores are *compelled or misled* by their assumption that the earth is very old; in other words, whether their preexisting belief about the age of the earth causes them to "see" 110,000 annual layers where there are fewer. We will focus our discussion of ice layer science on these two criticisms.

I. DO THE MARKERS INDICATE ANNUAL ICE LAYERS?

The first criticism is about how layers in an ice core are counted. How can we know that the layers each represent a year of time? There are at least four markers to consider.

First, the summer snow layers are composed mainly of fluffy snow called *hoar*. The daytime air warms the upper surface, causing new-fallen snow to thin from evaporation. Overnight the moist air resettles from the fog, forming additional light frost. The result: fine-grained new snow becomes coarse-grained, low density "hoar" about twice its original depth. The pockets in hoary snow will become large air bubbles as the layer becomes ice when it is compacted; thus these summer layers scatter light and are bright when backlit. In contrast, since the sun does not shine in the Arctic during the winter, the winter layers are mostly free of hoar. They are smoother and appear dark when backlit (see Figure 6.1). Multiple people work on counting these layers by hand.[8]

Second, warm summer air on the ocean surface causes a higher ratio of water containing *oxygen–18* to evaporate and fall as snow. The oxygen–18 is chemically the same as normal oxygen–16 but has two more neutrons and thus is physically heavier. Heavier water (H_2O) takes more energy to evaporate into the air; hence summer heat leads to a higher ratio of heavy oxygen in the snowfall. Scientists measure the O–18 and O–16 with a mass spectrometer.

Third, late-winter and spring winds in the northern hemisphere carry *dust* that settles over Greenland with the summer snow. The calmer fall winds bring less dust, on average. It is possible to measure the dust level in an ice layer by melting it and shining a light through the water using laser-light scattering (LLS).

Fourth, all snow contains numerous acids. The largest source is *nitric acid*, created by sunlight in our atmosphere.

The summer snow over Greenland contains higher nitric acid; winter snow averages less. Other acids show up nonseasonally, notably sulfuric and hydrochloric acids from occasional volcanic eruptions. Since acids are conductive, scientists measure the dissolved acids by applying a voltage across the ice using the electrical conductivity method (ECM). This technique works best for ice without cracks.

Concerns about these seasonal signals are raised in many publications by young-earth meteorologists. We will refer to two in this essay, Larry Vardiman and Michael Oard. For example, Michael Oard argues that "seasonal" markers occur multiple times a year due to storms and other nonseasonal events, especially in the deeper ice layers:

> Storms can cause depth hoar layers if the temperature gradient is sufficient during the changes between warm and cold sectors of storms. [These] can usually be counted as annual layers in the top portion of the GISP2. . . .
>
> In [our] compressed Creation/Flood model, with much thicker annual layers during the Ice Age, the dust represents an extremely dusty atmosphere . . . Storms would be very dirty and multiple bands of dust could be deposited on the ice sheet by several mechanisms. . . .
>
> There are many sources for sulfuric and nitric acids, which can vary with time and complicate the seasonal cycle. For instance, the nitrogen cycle in the atmosphere is highly complex with a number of variables affecting the nitrate and nitric acid generation that end up in the ice.[9a]

To emphasize that his criticism is valid, Oard quotes the writing of the team in charge of the visual dating on the GISP2 core, which was led by scientist Richard Alley. In a section of the primary publication, which is entitled "Sources

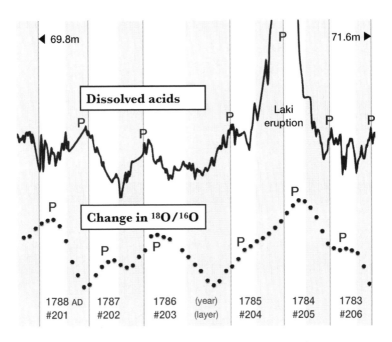

Fig. 6.2 GISP2 seasonal markers, 201 layers down. Dark/light vertical bands are the countable hoar layers (dark for winter). Dissolved acid peaks near the end of summer, and heavy oxygen peaks mid-summer (marked by P). Note the volcanic eruption in 1783 A.D. (Laki, Iceland).

of Error in Visible Stratigraphy," Alley wrote:

> Fundamentally, in counting any annual marker, we must ask whether it is absolutely unequivocal, or whether non-annual events could mimic or obscure a year. For the visible strata (and, we believe, for any other annual indicator at accumulation rates representative of central Greenland), it is almost certain that variability exists at the sub-seasonal or storm level, at the annual level and for various longer periodicities (2-year, sunspot, etc). We certainly must entertain the possibility of misidentifying the deposit of a large storm or a snow dune as an entire year or

missing a weak indication of a summer and thus picking a 2-year interval as 1 year.[10]

What can we say about these uncertainties? Is it a make-or-break issue if storms mimic annual cycles? I propose that we see for ourselves. In this case, the entire raw dataset of the GISP2 core is available online. So (naturally), I have taken the time personally to obtain the individual measurements made by the GISP2 team and to chart and analyze them for myself.[11]

In Figure 6.2, you see my own diagram of the dissolved acid and heavy oxygen ratios, shown against a gray+white background which represents Alley's physical count of hoar layers. This diagram comes from 69 meters down in the ice core. It spans layers #201–206 when counting *down from layer 1*, which starts in 1989 A.D.[12] Despite the noisy signal, you can see that the acid and oxygen levels each have summer peaks as they are viewed against the hoar layers. Even more interesting is the massive acid peak in layer #205. This corresponds to a nearby volcanic eruption at Mount Laki, Iceland in 1783–1784 A.D.—which was exactly 205(!) years prior to 1989, if you do the math. In fact, scientists have found multiple known volcanic eruptions to validate the layer count over the last few hundred years. Unique *volcanic ash* markers from a dozen historic eruptions in the previous 2,000 years confirm older layers as well—for example, Mt. Vesuvius in 79 A.D. (layer #1910).[13]

To check the accuracy of the layer counts that were included with this data, I also tried my own layer counting. Using the full acid chart, I counted the peaks several times from the top down to the Laki layer, averaging 203 to 206 peaks each time. As noted in Figure 6.2, the historical prediction is 205—thus it is clear to me that acid cycles really do represent an annual signal.[14] The same is true for heavy oxygen. Moreover, you can visually see that each bright summer layer begins where one is expected.

Do you agree that we can conclude—reasonably—that short-term weather events did not change the annual layer count at this depth in the ice core? Storms may be visible on the chart as smaller spikes, but they did not affect my counting of broad yearly trends. Furthermore, we can confirm the count to roughly 2,000 years ago using known volcanic eruptions. We are confident in the result because we see *agreement between multiple, diverse measurements.*

Here is Alley's conclusion, which follows his quote above but—surprisingly—is never mentioned in Oard's criticism:

> Where similar care has been taken in ice cores with a sufficiently high accumulation rate, zero-error ages also are obtained based on intercomparison and calibration to historical volcanic eruptions . . . particularly when the presence of tephra [i.e., volcanic ash] can verify the aerosol signal.

Thus the GISP2 team believes the annual ice layers are countable. Why? Because the uncertainty introduced from multiple storms per year is minimal, as evidenced by cross-checking the counted layers with known dates for volcanic eruptions. Moreover (although you do not get this impression from a quick reading of Vardiman or Oard), both young-earth scientists agree! Vardiman writes, "It is true that annual layers can be counted downward in Greenland through several thousand layers . . . but probably has little merit below several thousand layers."[15]

The next question is optional and will take longer to read. For group discussions, readers will find it helpful to skip to the next section. This will not disrupt the flow of the essay.

II. DOES BELIEF THAT THE EARTH IS VERY OLD DISTORT HOW A SCIENTIST COUNTS THE LAYERS?

It appears that the real point of contention is over the deeper layers in the ice. Ice core scientists do assume the Greenland ice sheet is very old—certainly more than 6,000 years. So Oard and Vardiman argue that this belief leads the GISP2 team to make a wrong assumption: that weather patterns were similar in the past. In other words, ice core scientists count or estimate the age in deeper layers even when they should not.

As an alternative, Vardiman proposes a climate model which makes a very different assumption about the weather: that the Ice Age was a rapid, high-precipitation event from about 2700 to 2000 B.C. caused by a massive climate change after Noah's Flood. This would change the way we count the deeper ice layers. He reasons:

> The conventional *long-age model* has dramatically expanded the time frame of the ice accumulation near the bottom. It will be necessary for the *recent-creation model* to carefully compress the time frame of the ice accumulation near the bottom of the cores to match my assumed Flood date.[16]

In this 700-year 'rapid' Ice Age (the *recent-creation model*), Vardiman proposes that large snowstorms laid down the

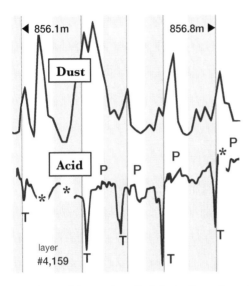

Fig. 6.3 More seasonal GISP2 markers. Vertical bands are the countable hoar layers (dark for winter, light for summer).

a. *Top left:* part of the "brittle ice" section of the core, starting 4,159 layers down. Dust peaks appear in mid-summer. Some of the acid data points are discontinuous (*), but show flat peaks in summer (P), and deep lows (T) in late winter.

b. *Bottom left*: another "brittle ice" section of the core, 7,142 layers down. Dust peaks appear in summer. Dissolved acid measurements are discontinuous (*), but have lows (T) in late winter, peaks (P) in summer. There is a high dust anomaly in the middle (a single point).

c. *Bottom right:* a deeper section of the core, 23,146 layers down. Dust peaks appear in summer. Dissolved acid shows peaks in late summer.

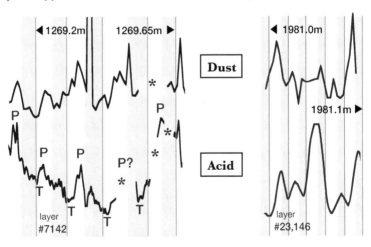

lower half of the Greenland ice sheet, becoming thousands of additional ice layers. (In context, it is a bit ironic that Vardiman seeks to reinterpret the ice layers to match his pre-existing assumption about the date of Noah's Flood.) But here again, we can take a look for ourselves.

In Figure 6.3, you see my diagram of dust levels and dissolved acids, shown again with the gray+white backdrop of Alley's hoar layer count.[17] I chose 856 meters and 1,269 meters for two reasons. First, they represent two sections of brittle/cracked ice where we can see an excellent example of the uncertainties in the data. Second, the layers in these are countable to 4,090 and 7,190 layers deep, respectively. This section of the ice is after Vardiman's proposed 'rapid' Ice Age (i.e., the layers are more recent).

Finally, I chose 1,981 meters because it was the deepest section counted *before* the GISP2 team made adjustments to their instruments. Due to the ever-thinning layers, the LLS laser beam was made narrower to measure dust below this depth. This was an unsurprising adjustment, but Oard contends that the increase in resolution would show false layers.[18] Thus for simplicity, I have chosen 1,981 meters, which also happens to be near the middle of the proposed 'rapid' Ice Age. (Nonetheless, this section of the ice is still 23,147 layers deep!)

At all three depths in Figure 6.3, you can see that the ice layers show the familiar match between hoar lines, dust,

---

Note on Figure 6.3c At this depth the GISP2 scientists began recording the hoar layers in units of ten, since they are less than an inch thick; so I have *generated* the dark/light layer markers on my diagram by evenly spacing them between the tens markers.

and acid peaks. Despite cracks in the brittle ice that sometimes hinder electrical conductivity (ECM), we see enough
cycles in the acid signal to make out a trend that follows the
seasons. The cycle is clear across all three markers. In fact,
I charted the markers at many other depths, even when one
of the data sets is unavailable.[19] The result is always the
same: the visual hoar layers match the measured markers.

Despite this compelling demonstration, Vardiman and
Oard argue that the deeper layers include many storm
cycles that *only look* like yearly cycles. So how can we triple-
verify which explanation is more likely? Are the data points
years or storms? Focusing our approach even further, how
can we check for confirmation?

To do this, I would like to look at one more chart. In
Figure 6.4, I have charted the thickness of every ice layer
for every data point down to layer #10,000. Each data
point is a dot. The gray dashed line represents the thickness predicted by the 'rapid' Ice Age model (see source in
endnote).[20] At the very top of the ice sheet, you can see the
measured layers range from 0.20–0.45 m thick. Then the
layers—progressively and consistently—become thinner at
greater depths. This is because the glacier ice behaves
much like a plastic material, and under pressure the deep
ice compresses and spreads out. You can also see that the
layer thicknesses from our earlier charts fit nicely within
this range (labeled 6.2, 6.3a, and 6.3b). The data point for
6.3c is located to the lower right (too far to display on the
page), and its location is consistent with the rest of the chart.

In contrast, Vardiman and Oard argue that the ice layer
thicknesses will be fairly constant between 0 m and 1500 m
deep (trace the dashed line in Figure 6.4).[9b] But as you can see

by the trend of data in the chart, *none of them* behave like this. Most importantly, Vardiman and Oard also predict *3-meter thick* annual ice layers during the 'rapid' Ice Age itself. The chart demonstrates this would only be true if every one of the data points deeper than layer #8000 has been misinterpreted as annual by the GISP2 team.

So are the deepest data points (to the right of layer #8000 in Figure 6.4) actually storm layers? Were they misinterpreted? I think the reasonable answer is: only if such storms have the *same expected thickness and matching markers* as the annual layers we verified for the shallow layers (to the left of layer #8000). Now, I cannot guess whether storms leave the same three seasonal markers in the snow as a yearly cycle, along with the same range of

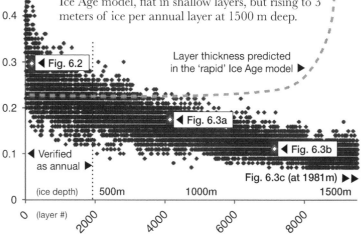

Fig. 6.4 Ice layer thicknesses plotted by layer number in the GISP2 ice core. Deeper layers are increasingly thin. Black dots are the measured thicknesses. The gray dotted line is a predicted thickness from the 'rapid' Ice Age model, flat in shallow layers, but rising to 3 meters of ice per annual layer at 1500 m deep.

thickness (m)

0.4

0.3   ◀ Fig. 6.2   Layer thickness predicted
                           in the 'rapid' Ice Age model ▶

0.2
                           ◀ Fig. 6.3a

0.1   ◀ Verified   ◀ Fig. 6.3b
      as annual ▶
                                    Fig. 6.3c (at 1981m) ▶▶

0   (ice depth)   500m   1000m   1500m

O (layer #)   2000   4000   6000   8000

3 m

thicknesses. Others say this is not the case.[21] But based on our survey of the data here, I do know it is *extremely unlikely*. It is difficult to believe that thousands of storm layers could seamlessly and invisibly replace the verified annual layers in our chart. The data does not allow us to conclude that.

If we judge our prior assumptions about the ice core based on what we see in the data—the rule of testability—then we follow a path of reason like this:

> After verifying that the top 205 visible layers in the GISP2 core are annual layers, with independent seasonal markers that match the visual count, and with evidence that each ice layer is progressively thinner;

> And with historical confirmation that the first 2000 layers are also annual, with the same independent markers;

> And observing that layer #2001 behaves in the same way, and the next layer, and the next, down to layer #23,147 (and some distance beyond), with no detectable change in the characteristics of seasonal markers or layer thinning;

> It appears that these deeper layers of the GISP2 ice core are also annual snow layers.

The ice layers in Figure 6.2 and Figure 6.3 fit with expectations if they are yearly cycles. This remains true as we drill down further on the data. Therefore, it seems clear that our prior assumptions did not control our interpretation.

In summary, the scientists who count annual layers in the GISP2 ice core are not blindly driven by their belief that the earth is old. Rather, it appears that the data itself—despite its inherent uncertainties—points them and us to a natural conclusion. We are more confident in the result because of our focus on the details.

———————————————— continue ————————————————

Curiosity about the details

The scientific process calls us to be very inquisitive. We need to be excellent students of the natural world, which means being great question-askers. As we saw in our study of ice cores, the trait or discipline of *focus* is fundamental to this process of discovery.

Specifically, *focus* means that we ask narrower questions first, before we work out the broader questions. *Do ice layers in Greenland represent annual cycles of snow?* is a broad question. *Can the peaks of O–18 in the mass spectrograph be paired consistently with the bright and dark ice layers?* is a narrow question—one of many narrow questions to ask. And in time, these smaller details help us verify and piece together the larger story.

To have a better appreciation for this focused approach in modern science, we need to know a few things about scientific theories. So I want to discuss two key aspects of theories that relate to our discussion here.

QUALITY. What makes a scientific theory a *good* theory? When should we consider a theory successful? Scientists use numerous core values to judge theories, and we mentioned a few earlier. Here are some of the most common values:

Explanatory. A theory should explain the pattern we see in nature more easily or more accurately than any other theory. It explains more of the data and is preferable.

Predictive. A theory is able to make predictions of the data (whether it be known evidence or yet to be observed). It is a testable guide to natural behaviors.

Coherent. A theory does not have contradictions in its logic. It should not require "just so" or *ad hoc* explanations for unexplained anomalies. It is rational and coherent.

Testable. A theory is open to verification. It should be testable by others and is stated in such a way that it can be proven false by practical experimentation.

Unifying. The best theory joins together observations that were previously unconnected or unknown. It is broadly explanatory of many natural behaviors.[22]

Thus a theory is a broad framework that explains how something works or came to be. It is not simply a guess. A good theory will have several statements or equations to be tested. The five values above—that a theory is explanatory, predictive, coherent, testable, and unifying—help us judge whether that theory is successful.

In the case of the 'rapid' Ice Age proposal (part II in the previous section), we clearly ran into problems. It was *testable*; we compared it against multiple data sets. But the proposal was only partly *coherent*, since it requires a large assumption that the Flood caused an Ice Age, and it failed to *explain* or *predict* the data we looked at. Therefore it is not a very solid theory. Keep in mind that we did not disprove everything the young-earth scientists believe. Rather, by asking narrow questions about ice cores, what we did was to cast doubt on (or *falsify*) the idea of a 'rapid' Ice Age. We must be careful not to overstate what we learned. Of course, we did find a good line of evidence that the ice is older than 6,000 years. Figure 6.3 confirms at least 23,000 years (see footnote for an even deeper count).[18] And so far, we have no reason to doubt the stated age of 110,000 years for the ice sheet.

Other theories about a young ice sheet fall short as well. For example, people sometimes debate about the "Lost Squadron," a group of Air Force planes that crash-landed on the Greenland ice in 1942. The planes were abandoned on the ice, slowly buried in deep annual snowfall. In 1988, a team managed to locate the airplanes and raise one to the surface—through a vertical hole 75 meters deep! Surely, they concluded, the snow in Greenland accumulates much faster than ice core scientists claim? But this is just a failure to ask focused questions. Greenland is a large island; it has several climate zones. The "Lost Squadron" was abandoned on the high-precipitation coastline, but the GISP2 borehole is located 504 miles inland, at 10,500 feet

Fig. 6.5

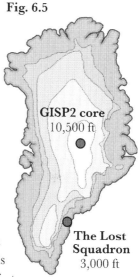

GISP2 core
10,500 ft

The Lost Squadron
3,000 ft

elevation on the low-precipitation summit (see Figure 6.5).[23] Asking focused questions gives us a clearer answer.

HISTORICAL SCOPE. What things can we theorize about nature, past and present? That may seem like a surprising question to ask, but there are a few people who choose to *reject all modern work* in paleosciences like geology and ice cores. Henry Morris, a young-earth advocate in the 20th century, wrote: "Science by definition necessarily can deal only with present processes."[24] Physical theories can be verified in a laboratory but historical events cannot be repeated, and therefore, he argued, theories about the past are untestable except when we use the Bible as our guide.

The Greenland ice sheet is an excellent counterexample to this concern. Glacier ice science involves *present-day* measurements as scientists return to the same locations each year and test the previous year's accumulation. Then, they compare ice layers in the *recent past* using the same markers and double-check these layers with known historical events. Finally, in layers from the *distant past*, they observe whether the same markers in the ice remain as consistent as in the recent layers. The science is the same at every stage —the same tools, measurements, and principles—but there is a seamless transition from present to past. So science is not simply a present endeavor.

What can we study, then? The answer is simple: we can study anything that allows us to ask questions, test, and make predictions of the data.

There are many aspects of focused science beyond the scope of this essay. For example, scientists in every field have procedures to limit personal bias. We need to understand them. I leave these as an exercise for you (the reader) to discover; it is worth our time to learn the details.

If we truly want to understand the natural world, we need the discipline of *focus*. We do this by asking questions and using methods that have a narrow, limited scope. In fact, if you or I need to make sense of scientific debates in the media, *focus* is the only way to go. It is how we make sense of the options and find truth. In the face of many uncertainties, we have confidence in the scientific process if we stick to our focus.

~

He determines the number of the stars
and calls them each by name.
Psalm 147:4

For discussion

1. What is something new that you learned in this essay?

2. How would you summarize the idea of *focus* as a key characteristic of science?

3. Are you concerned about the number of uncertainties that make science a challenge? Why or why not?

4. Proverbs 25:2 says, *"God delights in concealing things; scientists delight in discovering things" (The Message)*. Do you think this is a fair Christian motivation for practicing science? Why or why not?

5. Is it okay for scientists to make assumptions in their work? What assumptions are reasonable?

6. What are some ways that scientists can limit personal bias in their research?

7. What other values might be important to assess in a scientific theory, in addition to the five in this essay?

8. Reconstructing past events is the main task in fields such as archaeology, ice core science, and crime scene investigation (CSI). What controls or procedures might help us to trust the conclusions reached in these fields?

9. How much time are you able to give to research when you need to make up your mind on a scientific debate? What would make this process easier for you?

10. What role do you think the Bible should play, if any, in our study of Greenland ice cores?

[1] Basil of Caesarea, "The Creation of the Heavens and the Earth," trans. Agnes Clare Way, *Saint Basil: Exegetical Homilies*, 5.

[2] James Hutton, *Theory of the Earth, with Proofs & Illustrations*, 1.3.

[3] C. S. Lewis, *The Discarded Image*, 14–15.

[4] Karl Popper, *The Logic of Scientific Discovery*, 18–19.

[5] Howard Van Till, *Science Held Hostage: What's Wrong with Creation Science AND Evolutionism*, 36.

[6] For example, see the Tunu Ice Core Project blog, now archived at web.archive.org/web/*/http://icecores.blogs.dri.edu.

[7] Richard Alley and Sridhar Anandkrishnan, "Variations in melt-layer frequency in the GISP2 ice core: implications for Holocene summer temperatures in central Greenland," *Annals of Glaciology* 21: 65. Image source: wikimedia.org.

[8] Alley, *The Two Mile Time Machine*, 44.

[9] [a] Michael Oard, "Ice Cores vs. the Flood," *Journal of Creation (TJ)* 18, no. 2: 58–61. [b] See also Fig. 3 in Oard, "Do Greenland ice cores show over one hundred thousand years of annual layers?" *TJ* 15, no. 3, and Vardiman at icr.org/article/ice-cores-age-earth.

[10] Alley and others, "Visual-stratigraphic dating of the GISP2 ice core: Basis, reproducibility, and application," *Journal of Geophysical Research* 102, no. C12: 26,378.

[11] Data is from Earth Observing Laboratory, at data.eol.ucar.edu/codiac/dss/id=106.arcss008, with delta–O^{18} data from the QIL laboratory, archived at https://web.archive.org/web/20150826134957/http://depts.washington.edu/qil/datasets.

[12] The chart numbers come from the files visual.dat, m0050.dat, and b0050.dat. Note that 1989 is used as the zero year.

[13] Debra Meese and others, "The Greenland Ice Sheet Project 2 depth-age scale: Methods and results," *Journal of Geophysical Research* 102, no. C12: 26,412. See also Henrik Clausen, "A comparison of the volcanic records over the past 4000 years from the Greenland Ice Core Project and Dye 3 Greenland ice cores," *Journal of Geophysical Research* 102, no. C12: 26,715.

[14] A smoothing function in Microsoft Excel was applied to the data in order to eliminate false trends from single data points.

[15] Larry Vardiman, *Ice Cores and the Age of the Earth*, 33.

[16] Vardiman, 32. Italics are added for clarity.

[17] The heavy oxygen ratio is not available in fine increments below 300 m because the oxygen (as a gas) slowly diffuses between the layers and becomes indistinguishable over time.

[18] Oard, 60. In this case, scientists reduced the LLS beam width from 8 mm to 1 mm to measure layers at depths *below* 2300 m. Oard argues that using a higher resolution beam in order to reveal more layers only confirms the presupposition that more annual layers should be present. The scientists explain that a narrower beam is necessary to discern narrower layers as the ice layers become progressively thinner (i.e., the LLS adjustment is within expectations). See Meese, 26,419. Note the annual layers *above* 2300 m still add up to 42,393 years before present.

[19] See "Table 2" listing partial sections of data, in Meese, 26,413.

[20] From "Figure 3" in Oard, "Greenland," 41. Oard's chart is for the GRIP, a sister ice core about 30 km from the GISP2 core.

[21] See Richard Alley, "Concerning the Deposition and Diagenesis of Strata in Polar Firn," *Journal of Glaciology* 34: 283–90 (1988), and Paul Seely, "The GISP2 Ice Core: Ultimate Proof that Noah's Flood Was Not Global," *Perspectives on Science and Christian Faith* 55, no. 5: 252–260.

[22] Adapted from Ernan McMullin, "Values in Science," *Zygon* 47, no. 4: 698–699. See also Howard Van Till, *Portraits of Creation*, 141–145, and Del Ratzsch, *Science & Its Limits*, 69–70.

[23] GISP2 snow accumulation data at the summit is available at climatechange.umaine.edu/GISP2/data/accum.html. See also creation.com/the-lost-squadron and media.defense.gov/2017/Jun/27/2001769194/-1/-1/0/GreenlandPatrolIceCapRescueTaub2011.pdf.

[24] Henry Morris and John Whitcomb, *The Genesis Flood: the Biblical Record and its Scientific Implications*, xxvi.

7

Fidelity:
staying true to the biblical word

Think back to your life as a child. Do you remember a moment when someone taught you about your national heritage? Perhaps a parent explained the meaning of a founding document. Or maybe you remember when the national anthem or a famous speech became important to you. What were these experiences like for you? And how were those words or speeches explained to you at the time?

For myself (as a resident of the United States), the most powerful experience was learning our national anthem, *The Star-Spangled Banner*. Many times I remember when an athlete won against heavy odds in the Olympics and I felt a deep pride as we heard the national anthem at the medal ceremony. Those experiences were deep and unforgettable. Similar feelings wash over me at every Olympics. I am known to be teary-eyed whenever I hear the anthem or see the flag raised.

Interestingly, we spent very little time thinking about the words. I did know that Francis Scott Key wrote the lyrics to the anthem after the British shelled Fort McHenry. My parents and teachers explained why "the land of the free and the home of the brave" was important: the loss of our national independence was at stake in the War of 1812. This helped me understand why Key rejoiced when he saw the flag at "dawn's early light": the battle was not lost, and our national freedom remained. But we did not analyze the words too closely beyond that.

Did you know that *The Star-Spangled Banner* does not tell the fullest story of the flag? In fact, we misunderstand the poem if we assume it contains accurate historical details. At first glance, the lyrics refer to a single flag: the one that Key saw flying above the fort (Figure 7.1). But it turns out there were actually *two* physical flags. The flag in the first line would be the fort's main garrison flag, taken down before the battle because of rain and raised again at dawn. This is the flag on display in the Smithsonian. The flag seen in "the rockets' red glare," however, was a smaller storm flag that flew at night during the attack. Fine distinctions like this make poor poetry and do not matter to the audience; so Key's lyrics simply refer to the two flags as "our flag," as if there were only one.[2]

Moreover, there is actually a *third* flag at the end of the stanza! Do you see it? It is a symbolic flag—the representation of freedom that lives in the hearts of Americans. We know this because of the rhetorical question and the universality of the words in the final phrase: "O say does that star-spangled banner yet wave...?" Because the flag is a symbol, *The Star-Spangled Banner* inspires people today as

O say can you see by the dawn's early light what so proudly we hail'd at the twilight's last gleaming, whose broad stripes & bright stars through the perilous fight o'er the ram-parts we watch'd, were so gallantly streaming?

And the rockets' red glare, the bombs bursting in air, gave proof through the night that our flag was still there; *O say does that star-spangled banner yet wave o'er the land of the free and the home of the brave?*

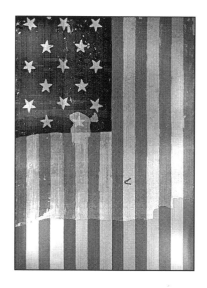

Fig. 7.1 The Fort McHenry garrison flag with the first stanza of *The Star-Spangled Banner*, written by Francis Scott Key in 1814.[1]

much as it did when it was written. In brief, vivid words, it tells our national story of origin.

What shall we conclude? First, the words of the anthem are not mere historical references. Some are also symbolic. And second, the words obscure their reference points and so cannot be used to answer detailed historical questions about the battle. The anthem glosses over how many flags were at Fort McHenry. Various other markers in the text (rhyming, imagery, and rhetorical questions) point us to what the poet meant to say. So the anthem's true meaning is indicated by the *way* the words are used.

I am not splitting hairs here. The way we should treat *The Star-Spangled Banner* is not how many people treat the

Scripture, especially as it relates to science. Sometimes we expect more historical and scientific accuracy from the Bible than is actually present. Instead, we must strive for faithfulness—or *fidelity*—to the true purposes of Scripture.

The Bible is the most diverse collection of writings that you or I will ever read. There may be one Divine voice, but there are also many human voices. With each verse, we should ask: *What is the main point of these words?* and seek to discover each author's form, style, and intentions. This is our first goal whenever we pick up a Bible.

Here are some past theologians writing about the idea of purpose or intention in Scripture:

(Please refer to primary sources on the next page.)

1) John Stott, a pastor and theologian in the 20th century, argued that the purpose of the Bible is to transform and redeem human beings. All other aspects of its writings are secondary, including its scientific accuracy. Each Scripture should be interpreted, first and foremost, in light of how it speaks about salvation and the spiritual situation of humanity.

2) Henri Blocher, an Old Testament scholar, emphasized the vast diversity of language available to biblical authors. In ancient life (just as in our modern world), words and larger forms of speech were flexible. Depending on the context, they could be used with varying levels of "literal-ness." Therefore an interpreter needs to know the genre of a Bible passage to understand its intent.

3) N. T. Wright, a New Testament scholar, writes that the word *literal* originally meant "the sense of the letter"—

ON INTENTION IN SCRIPTURE

John Stott, in *Understanding the Bible* (1982):

> The Bible is primarily a book neither of science, nor of literature, nor of philosophy, but of salvation. In saying this we must give the word "salvation" its broadest possible meaning. Salvation is far more than merely the forgiveness of sins. It includes the whole sweep of God's purpose to redeem and restore humankind, and indeed all creation. What we claim for the Bible is that it unfolds God's total plan.
>
> It begins with the creation, so that we may know the divine likeness in which we were made, the obligations which we have repudiated and the heights which we have fallen. . . . The main thrust of the biblical message [is] that God loves the very rebels who deserve nothing at his hand but judgment. Before time began, Scripture says, his plan of salvation took shape.[3]

Henri Blocher, in *In the Beginning* (1984):

> Human speech rarely remains at the zero point of plain prose, which communicates in the simplest and most direct manner, using words in their ordinary sense. The word acquires very varied effects by taking off from this lowest point . . . These are ways of speaking, turns of phrase, which distort language to a greater or lesser degree — the listener, of course, must take this into account, if he is not to mistake the meaning in a comic, or sometimes tragic, way. Herod is a fox only metaphorically (Lk. 13:32) . . .
>
> But the figures of speech are not all so easily detected, nor are they all part of such small units of discourse. The adoption of a literary genre generally allows a step to be taken away from ordinary expression, from the zero point. Thus the reader will refuse to take 'literally' the seed and the Sower (Mt. 13:4-9), not because of anything in individual sentences, but because he knows he is reading a parable. The indications of the literary genre of the text affect its overall reading.[4]

ON INTENTION IN SCRIPTURE *continued*

N. T. Wright, in *The Last Word* (2005):

When the Reformers insisted on the "literal" sense of scripture, they were referring to the first of the four medieval senses [i.e., literal, allegorical, anagogical, moral]. Though, as we saw, this would often refer to the historical meaning and referent of scripture (when scripture says that Solomon's men built the Temple, for example, the literal sense is that Solomon's men built the Temple), the "literal" sense actually means "the sense of the letter"; and if the "letter"—the actual words used by the author or editors—is metaphorical, so be it. Thus, confusingly for us perhaps, the "literal" sense of Psalm 18:88, which speaks of smoke coming out of God's nostrils, is that, by this rich metaphor, the Psalmist is evoking the active and terrifying indignation of the living God against those who oppress his people.[5]

Eugene Peterson, in *Eat This Book* (2009):

There is a sense in which the Scriptures are the word of God dehydrated, with all the originating context removed — living voices, city sounds, camels carrying spices from Seba and gold from Ophir snorting down in the bazaar, fragrance from lentil stew simmering in the kitchen — all now reduced to marks on thin onion-skin paper. We make an effort at rehydrating them; we take these Scriptures and spend an hour or so in Bible study with friends or alone in prayerful reading. But five minutes later, on our way to work, plunged into the tasks of the day for which they had seemed to promise sustenance, there's not much left of them — only ink on india paper. We find that we are left with the words of the Bible but without the world of the Bible. Not that there is anything wrong with the words, as such, it is just that without the biblical world — the intertwined stories, the echoing poetry and prayers, Isaiah's artful thunder and John's extravagant visions — the words, like those seed words in Jesus' parable that land on pavement or in gravel or among weeds, haven't taken root in our lives.[6]

the sense intended by the author. A literal interpretation (in our modern sense) is not necessarily the literal meaning. A metaphorical, figurative, or plain statement is the "literal" meaning if it is intended by the writer. The modern definition of *literal* is unrealistically narrow.

4) Eugene Peterson, a pastor-theologian and the translator of *The Message*, reminds us to be fully immersed in the life-giving Scripture. We need to appreciate the sights, smells, sounds, and situations of its ancient hearers when we read it. Having the "words" without the "world" of the Bible leaves us with an impoverished understanding of its purpose.

These four viewpoints illustrate some of the practices of faithful interpretation. How do we discover the purpose of a Bible passage? We consider its theology, its written form, and its literal sense or usage. We also try to appreciate how it "comes to life." These practices guide our interpretation. Moreover, they help us decide when a passage is making concrete scientific or historical statements.

The starting point is to discover the *genre* of a biblical passage. And what is *genre*? It is the category of writing, such as poetry, parable, or legal code. In a sense, the genre determines the rules for interpretation: it tells us how the words are to be used. And each genre has its own unique markers. For example, if a story starts with *Once upon a time*, we would expect a morality play and not a history. Or if we hear *A priest, a rabbi, and a donkey walk into a bar* (or any combination of three strange nouns), we know to laugh at the exaggerations without taking offense.

The written markers are a cue to the audience about

the genre of the text. But it is also common for readers to miss these markers. In my experience, this is especially true for Christians. It takes more work to be objective when a person is already familiar with the Bible.

To this end, I have chosen a case study so we can observe how to maintain fidelity in a biblical genre. Our topic is an area of historical interest: genealogies in Genesis. Then we will look at some key aspects of biblical interpretation.

Case study on *fidelity*: Genesis 5 & 11 genealogies

Many older Bibles include a date at the top of each page. The most striking of these is the year 4004 B.C. which often decorates Genesis 1:1. In 1650, Anglican bishop James Ussher calculated this date by adding up the genealogies in Genesis 5 and 11 and connecting them to known historical dates elsewhere in the Bible. He famously concluded that Creation began at twilight on October 23, 4004 B.C.[7]

Other people over the centuries have devised similar chronologies with the genealogies. But most commentaries on Genesis do not consider this calculation valid, nor will you find a date for Genesis 1:1 in modern translations of the Bible. Many contemporary theologians suggest that the genealogies in Genesis 5 and 11 are not intended to be used as accurate-to-the-year histories. Why?

Today, the purpose of a family tree is to save a complete record of our relationships and their timeline. But ancient genealogies had very different functions: to demonstrate blessings, establish privileges, draw theological contrasts, or make statements about God's character. Thus they take different forms in the Bible to fit these purposes.

Linear genealogies establish a long line to an individual's key ancestors. It is not uncommon for linear genealogies to skip generations so that the form has proper emphasis or balance. Matthew 1:8 lists Azariah/Uzziah as the "son" of Joram, omitting three generations (versus 1 Chronicles 3:11) in order to show Jesus' lineage in equal sections of fourteen. The abbreviated genealogy in Ezra 7:3 omits six names in a single generation (versus 1 Chronicles 6:7–10).[8]

On the other hand, *segmented genealogies* establish a broad connection between family members and their domain of influence. They are selective as well. Genesis 10:16–18 lists some sons of Shem, Ham, and Japheth to the sixth generation, but others only to the second. It lists their seventy descendants—a number of totality—in which some names are not individuals at all, but nations![9]

Genesis 5:3–32 and 11:10–26 are both linear genealogies. Each lists ten descendants (Adam to Noah, and Shem to Abram, respectively), with the final generation containing three sons.[10] Moreover, Genesis 5 follows Seth's line and makes note of Enoch's godly life in the seventh generation. This parallels the prior genealogy in Genesis 4, which follows Cain's line and ends with Lamech's curse in the seventh generation. The lines of Adam's two sons are in sharp contrast. So it seems that theology and symmetry, rather than historical completeness, drive the forms of Genesis 5 and 11. If so, these chapters make important statements about people but are not assumed to list every person. Bruce Waltke, an Old Testament theologian, adds:

> [The genealogies] have an unknown number of gaps. They function to show either that the last named person is a descendant of the first named person or to show the relationships of people, not to compute the age of the earth.[11]

It is important to note that the genealogies in Genesis 5 and 11 are unique in the Bible. They use the formula, *lived X years and begot a son, lived Y years afterward*, which is not used elsewhere. This phrase leaves plenty of room for some to reject the idea that Genesis 5 and 11 have any gaps. These criticisms come from stronger advocates of biblical literalism who believe that the genealogies are complete and should be used to mark the date of Creation roughly 6,000 years ago.

It is impossible here to describe every criticism raised. But my synopsis is that the criticisms center on two main issues: (1) whether the ages in the formulas are intended to be numerical and historically "additive"; and (2) whether the word "begot" (Hebrew *yalad*) can be used to indicate a distant descendant, skipping generations. We will focus our discussion of genealogies on these two criticisms.

I. ARE THE AGES INTENDED TO BE NUMERICAL?

How are numbers used in the Old Testament to count years? There are at least three cases to consider.

First, numbers are often meant literally by the author. Thus Exodus 12:41 states that Israel lived in Egypt for 430 years "to the day." Likewise, the reigns of Israel's kings are very detailed and additive. And since Genesis 5 and 11 both use the formula, *lived X years/lived Y years* (Figure 7.2), a natural possibility is that they are also additive. Years ago, Gerhard Hasel coined a word to describe this viewpoint:

> In view of this unique phenomenon we must be careful not to interpret the nature of the lists in these two chapters in the same way as in the [other] genealogies . . . We suggest a designation that more accurately reflects the nature of the features of Genesis 5 and 11:10–26 by the choice of the name of ***chronogenealogy***.[12]

ומאת שנים חמש שת־ויחי
And lived Seth five years & a hundred

:אנוש־את ויולד שנה
years and begot >> Enosh.

ויחי ־ שת אחרי הולידו
And lived Seth after (he) begot

שנים שבע אנוש־את
>> Enosh seven years

ויולד שנה מאות ושמנה
and eight hundred years and begot

:ובנות בנים
sons and daughters.

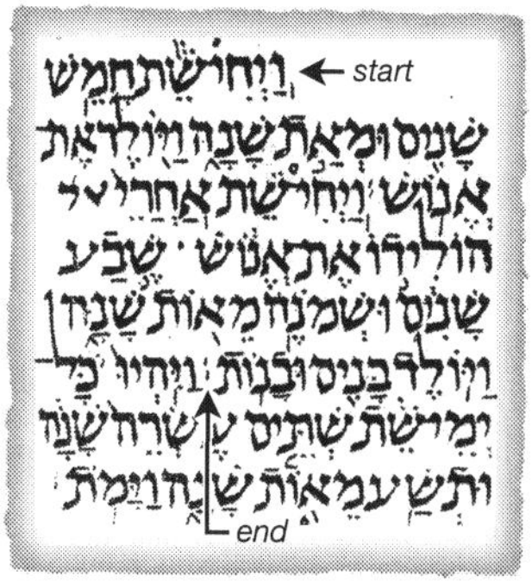

Fig. 7.2 Genesis 5:6–7 is a linear genealogy of Adam's son, Seth. See Figure 7.4 for explanatory notes.

Second, numbers are sometimes rounded. Most of us are not bothered that Israel was prophesied to be in Egypt for 400 years, not 430 years, in Genesis 15:13. We know that Abram's vision has a different purpose. Likewise, Gideon's army was reduced to 10,000, and then to 300, in Judges 7. The Hebrews often used round numbers in their record-keeping and story-telling. Thus genealogical values might be rounded as well. This could explain why some X/Y ages in Genesis 5 and 11 are multiples of a hundred.

Third, numbers may be symbolic and carry a non-numerical meaning. That is, ancient readers did not care about the literal value, in the same way that modern people know that the *10 million dollar question* is simply the most important question, or that *adding your 2 cents* means to give an opinion. Such numbers have culturally-defined meanings. So consider what one scientist has to say about

	GENESIS 5	AGE X	AGE Y		GENESIS 11	AGE X	AGE Y
1	**Adam**	130	800	11	**Shem**	100	500
2	**Seth**	105	807	12	**Arphaxad**	35	403
3	**Enosh**	90	815	13	**Shelah**	30	403
4	**Kenan**	70	840	14	**Eber**	34	430
5	**Mehalalel**	65	830	15	**Peleg**	30	209
6	**Jared**	162	800	16	**Reu**	32	207
7	**Enoch**	65	300	17	**Serug**	30	200
8	**Methuselah**	187	782	18	**Nahor**	29	119
9	**Lamech**	182	595	19	**Terah**	70	135
10	**Noah**	500	450	20	**Abram**		

Fig. 7.3 A table of the "chronogenealogies" in Genesis 5 and 11. *Age X* shows the father's age at the birth of his first-born son. *Age Y* shows the remaining years he lived until death. Note that Abraham is the completion point of the lineage and his ages are not listed by the author here. Gray boxes in the second genealogy indicate ages that do not end in the pattern 0/2/5/7.

the curious *X/Y* age "data" in Genesis 5 (see Figure 7.3):

> If one of my graduate students included the table in a paper and I published it, I would be censured. The verdict would be immediate and unquestioned—because the data are clearly fabricated. Why do I say this? Because the first two columns are not random in the last digit.[13]

In other words, all twenty of the *X/Y* pairs in Genesis 5 end in the digits 0, 2, 5, or 7. Since human beings live to be random ages, this outcome is impossible. There is a 40% chance that a random number will have a final digit of 0, 2, 5, or 7, but only a 40%-to-the-twentieth-power chance that twenty such numbers end in these digits. Even if we allow any combination of four digits (not just 0/2/5/7), the likelihood of this outcome is only *1 in 433,093.*[14] The conclusion? The ages in Genesis 5 do not represent literal human ages—they have been chosen to fit a pattern. To a lesser degree, we also see this in Genesis 11.

Why this pattern? An important paper by geologist Carol Hill argues that these numbers are a harmony of the Mesopotamian sacred number 60 (in years or months), and the sacred number 7. Some examples:

Adam	130	= 60×2 years + 60×2 months
	800	= (60×100 + 60×60) months
Seth	105	= (60×10×2 + 60) months
	807	= Adam's 800 years + 7 years
Enoch	65	= 60 years + 60 months
	300	= 60×60 months
Noah	500	= 60×100 months
	450	= (60×100 − 60×10) months

All ages ending in 0/2/5/7 are similar. Thus Hill writes:

> One of the religious considerations of the ancients involved in numbers was to make certain that any numbering scheme worked out numerologically; i.e., that it used, and added up to, the right numbers symbolically. This is distinctively different from a secular use of numbers in which the overriding concern is that numbers add up to the correct total arithmetically. . . . The sacred numbers used by the Mesopotamians gave a type of religious dignity or respect to important persons.[15]

Of course, numbers can have many interesting features, but not all of them are intended by the author or relevant. Here is a great question to ask: *Is this pattern meaningful to the audience?* In other words, does the pattern serve a purpose?

It turns out that there are two good precedents for symbolic numbers in these genealogies.

First of all, Abram and his ancestors came from Mesopotamia. The setting in Genesis 2–11 is Mesopotamian, unlike the nomadic, Semitic world we see in Genesis 12–50 after Abram settles in Canaan. The genealogies likely reflect Mesopotamian culture and its unique use of numbers.[16]

And secondly, symbolic numbers appear throughout the Old Testament. For example, God took Enoch away at 365 years old—a statement about a complete "year" or season. Joseph died in Egypt at 110 years old—a perfect age in the Egyptian culture which some commentators believe is an epitaph about a highly-respected life.[17] Moses died at 120 years old *despite the fact* that "his eye was dimmed and his vigor unabated" (Deuteronomy 34:7). Since 120 is the lifespan allotted to humans in Genesis 6:3, this is a statement that Moses completed his calling and, like Enoch, was taken away. The numbers are first and foremost *numerological* (i.e., symbolic), so we cannot expect *numerical* accuracy from them.

Does it seem reasonable to conclude that the ages in Genesis 5 and 11 are not additive, at least in the way that we would write history today? Yes. Certainly the Genesis 5 and 11 formulas are unique. But the literal interpretation, as in Hasel's word *chronogenealogy*, does not make sense of the numbers themselves. The numbers do not have random characteristics like real ages. And rounding is also unlikely, since it is hard to imagine why numbers would ever be rounded to end in 2, 5, or 7. Therefore, the most likely option is that they are somehow symbolic—they indicate something other than an age.

> The next question is optional and will take longer to read. For group discussions, readers will find it helpful to skip to the next section. This will not disrupt the flow of the essay.

II. Does the Word 'Begot' Skip Generations?

The second concern in Genesis 5 and 11 is the meaning of the Hebrew word *yalad*, or "begot" in older English translations. Contemporary Bibles translate the word as *fathered, became the father of, bore,* or *gave birth to,* depending on their gender. To be clear, the main issue is *not* whether genealogies can skip generations. Scholars of all persuasions agree that they sometimes do. But all such genealogies use the Hebrew word *ben*, or "son," in the formula: *C, son of B, son of A.* So the real concern is the unique use of the word *yalad*/"begot" found in the genealogies of Genesis 5 and 11. A strong criticism comes from Larry Pierce and Ken Ham:

> Nowhere in the Old Testament is the Hebrew word for begat (*yalad*) used in any other way than to mean a single-generation (e.g., father/son or mother/daughter) relationship. The Hebrew word *ben* can mean *son* or *grandson*, but the word *yalad* never skips generations.[18]

What can we say about this? Is *yalad* ever used to indicate more than a single generation? I propose that we see for ourselves. In this case, old Hebrew manuscripts are available online as digital scans. So (naturally), I have taken time to obtain the primary manuscript, the *Leningrad Codex*, that is used for all Old Testament translations today.[19]

Fig. 7.4 At right is the scan of the Masoretic text of the Old Testament, the *Leningrad Codex*. The start and end of the section are marked by arrows. At left is my literal translation in English. I have reordered the words from left to right for English readers. The direct object marker, את (or ואת), is written as ">>".

a. Genesis 46:18. The summary of the segmented genealogy of Zilpah, concubine of Leah (Jacob's wife). Zilpah's two direct sons were listed with their descendants in the two verses prior. In this summary verse, the direct object of the verb *yalad*/"begot" (line 3) is the pronoun "these" (line 3) of whom the author indicates is a total of sixteen people. The noun "sons" (line 1) also refers to the sixteen, since it is the antecedent of "these" (line 3).

אלה   אשר זלפה בני אלה־
These (are the) sons of Zilpah whom

בתו ללאה לבן נתן
gave Laban to Leah his daughter

ליעקב ותלד   אלה־את
and (she) begot >> these to Jacob

נפש עשרה שש
sixteen persons.

b. Genesis 10:15–16. A part of the segmented genealogy of Canaan, the grandson of Noah. The direct objects of the verb *yalad*/"begot" (line 1) are his son Sidon and Cheth, the Jebusites, Amorites, Girgashites, plus six more nations in verse 17 and 18. The symbol **:** after Cheth is a verse indicator added by the Jewish scribes; it does not indicate a new sentence.

בכרו צידן־את ילד וכנען
And Canaan begot >> Sidon his first

היבוסי ־ ואת :חת־ואת
and>> Cheth, and>> the Jebusites

:הגרגשי ואת האמרי־ואת
and>> the Amorites and>> the Girgashites

Looking back to Figure 7.2, we see an illustration from Genesis 5:6–7, which shows how *yalad* is used in the original text. Here the verb is followed by the direct object of its action. The order is *subject – verb – direct object*. A Hebrew word, את (*'et*), sits between the verb and its direct object in both locations. Scholars translate את as ">>" because it has no English equivalent. It is used in Hebrew to mark the direct object, like this: *Seth begot >> Enosh*.[20] Can the word "begot" indicate a broader step than from parent to child? We need to know how the word is used in similar contexts to be sure. This will help us to understand its meaning and keep fidelity to the Word. Let us look at three examples.

First of all, a brief genealogy in Genesis 46:16–18 lists the family of Jacob's concubine, Zilpah. Both of her sons, Gad and Asher, are named along with the grandsons they produced. Two great-grandsons are also listed. The final verse summarizes the genealogy using *yalad*:

> The sons of Gad: Ziphion, Haggi, Shuni, Ezbon, Eri, Arodi, and Areli. The sons of Asher: Imnah, Ishvah, Ishvi, Beriah, with Serah their sister. And the sons of Beriah: Heber and Malchiel. These are the sons of Zilpah, whom Laban gave to Leah his daughter; and these she bore [*yalad*] to Jacob—sixteen persons.

Here is the pressing question: does *yalad* refer to Gad and Asher or to the entire clan? Pierce and Ham argue:

> The context makes it very clear that Zilpah had only two sons, and this passage does not show that the Hebrew word *yalad* . . . implies a grandson, as well as a son.[21]

But as we see above and in Figure 7.4a, the object of *yalad* is the pronoun "these" in the summary verse. The author indicates this is a total of sixteen people. When we read the words in their Hebrew order, the sentence literally reads: "she_begot>>these_to_Jacob_sixteen_persons." Furthermore, when we look back for the noun that "these" refers to (i.e., its antecedent), we find "sons of Zilpah." Therefore *yalad* describes Zilpah's motherhood over the entire clan. Her "sons" total these sixteen people.

Second, the genealogy in Genesis 10:15–18 describes the descendants of Canaan. This list includes Canaan's two sons, Sidon and Cheth. Interestingly, it also includes the names of nine tribes and nations:

> Canaan fathered [*yalad*] Sidon his firstborn and Heth [i.e., Cheth], and the Jebusites, the Amorites, the Girgashites, the Hivites, the Arkites, the Sinites, the Arvadites, the Zemarites, and the Hamathites.

As we see in Figure 7.4b, the direct object marker for *yalad* is applied to Sidon, Cheth, and to each people group. The clear implication is that Canaan "begot" all of them, since there is no other verb in the list. In Hebrew order, it reads: "Canaan_begot>>Sidon_his_first_and>>Cheth_and>>the_ Jebusites_and>>the_Amorites_and>>the_Girgashites." And no grammatical distinctions are made between any of these names; they are treated as equal objects of the verb.

Third, part of a genealogy in Exodus 6:16–20 describes the descendants of Levi. This list focuses on the ancestors of Aaron and Moses, and it includes two important ages:

> [16] These were the names of the sons of Levi according to their records: Gershon, Kohath and Merari. . . .

> [18] The sons of Kohath were Amram, Izhar, Hebron and Uzziel. Kohath lived 133 years. . . .

> [20] Amram married his father's sister Jochebed, who bore him Aaron and Moses. Amram lived 137 years.

Interestingly, we know that Kohath came with the Hebrew families when they moved to Egypt during the great famine in the time of Joseph (Genesis 46:11). Taking this genealogy literally, Moses was born a *maximum* of $133+137 = 270$ years into the Egyptian captivity. But a careful reading shows that this math is impossible. How so?

Since Israel's captivity was 430 years, and Moses was 80 years old when Israel left Egypt (Exodus 7:7), we know that he was born $430–80 = 350$ years into the captivity. Thus the genealogy is missing 80 years (350–270), and *yalad* must gloss over several generations. In fact, Numbers 3:28 lists 8,600 descendants of Kohath during the time of the Exodus! So we have to assume that this genealogy is not a complete history.[22] Perhaps Amram was highlighted here because he married an aunt—a practice later disallowed under the Law. But most certainly Amram is *not* Moses' father, whose true parents are left anonymous in Exodus 2:1.

Moreover, the specific form of *yalad* in Genesis 5 and 11 is a causative form (in Hebrew: the *hiphil*).[23] It is not "Seth begot" but literally "Seth caused to beget." Although the verb is still translated the same way in English, the causative form distances the verb's action from its direct object (i.e., others could have participated in the process). This strengthens the case that *yalad*/"begot" is used as a broad term of relationship, like "son" or "father" is in other genealogies.

In summary, there is plenty of room in Genesis 5 and 11 for a condensed list of names. Genealogies that use *yalad*/ "begot" are not necessarily exhaustive. We can be more confident in this interpretation because of our fidelity to the words (and so the Word) of the written text.

—————————— continue ——————————

Fidelity to the words and Word

The interpretive process calls us to be very inquisitive. We need to be students of God's Word, which means being great question askers. As we saw in our study of Old Testament genealogies, the value or practice of *fidelity* guides us in this process of discovery.

Specifically, fidelity means that we remain true to the intent of the inspired, written text. This is a conviction to stand on. We ask questions like *What is the main point of these words?* and *What are the clues to help us understand them better?* And once we know how the words resonated in the ears, minds, and hearts of its listeners—what it meant and how it motivated the first audience—we will apply the Scripture accurately. Gordon Fee, the theologian who wrote *How to Read the Bible for All Its Worth*, asserts:

> The only proper control for hermeneutics [i.e., how we interpret the Bible] is to be found in the original intent of the biblical text. . . . The true meaning of the biblical text for us is what God originally intended it to mean when it was first spoken.[24]

Faithful study requires us to ask many things about a passage. Once we know its genre, we can ask additional questions about context, grammar, and rhetorical devices, which vary by genre. A poor thing to do, then, is to miss the point by mistaking the genre. For example, astronomer Hugh Ross uses the gaps in New Testament genealogies to imply that Genesis 5 and 11 have very large gaps—not just a few, but enough that Adam could have lived 30,000+ years ago.[25] But a genealogy in 1st century Palestine, such as in Matthew 1:1–17 or Luke 3:23–38, may have a different purpose than a much older genealogy that uses symbolic

Mesopotamian numbers. *Genealogy* is not a singular genre.

Besides genre, there are many other identifying markers that help us know the purpose of a Bible passage. I want to discuss three markers that relate to our discussion here.

DIRECT STATEMENTS. What does the author say about their purpose? Look carefully. For example, consider what John and Luke say about their gospels:

> John 20:31 — These [words] are written that you may believe that Jesus is the Messiah, the Son of God, and that by believing you may have life in his name.

> Luke 1:3–4 — Since I myself have carefully investigated everything from the beginning, I too decided to write an orderly account for you, most excellent Theophilus, so that you may know the certainty of the things you have been taught.

Thus John intends to strengthen the listener's life in Christ, whereas Luke aims to convince the listener that Jesus' story is true. Both authors write history—but both of them say they will do it differently.

As a result, the Gospel of John has a theological focus, not a chronological one. The events are ordered differently. John's gospel has a broad chronology, of course: it starts with Jesus' first miracle and ends with his crucifixion. But other events are not in order: Jesus cleanses the Temple at the beginning of his ministry, rather than during his final week as we read in the other gospels. In contrast, Luke's gospel maintains an accurate order. Those who miss the point of the two histories are forced to argue that Jesus cleansed the Temple twice! But it is sufficient to understand that ancient "history" does not follow modern rules. Simply put, John's purpose for his gospel is different than Luke's.

Old Testament authors make fewer direct statements about their purpose. But they often show their intentions in other ways, including through structure. Hebrew chiasm (*A-B-B'-A'*) and parallelism (*A-B|A'-B'*) are the two most common forms. For example, Genesis 1 employs a parallel between days 1–3 and 4–6. That knowledge helps us to answer the question, *How can light be separated from the darkness on Day 1 if the sun is not created until Day 4?* Because they are written in parallel, these two days are not separate events—they refer to the same event. We see *that* God separated the light from the darkness on Day 1 (Genesis 1:4). Then we see *how* it happened on Day 4 (Genesis 1:18), where it is the sun and moon that "separate light from darkness."

CULTURAL NORMS. What can we learn from how Bible passages follow cultural norms? Specific words, structures, symbols, or grammar are used in formulaic ways in each type of writing. For example, Old Testament covenants follow the pattern of ancient treaties (Genesis 15). And symbols such as the tree of life (Genesis 2) or the ocean of chaos (Genesis 1) are found in other Near Eastern origin stories. Understanding each norm—especially how each author uses or bends the norm—is the way we know when something important is being said.

The distinction between norm and purpose is helpful when we read historical narratives. The stories in Genesis 1–11 have a pre-historic, timeless style similar to Egyptian and Mesopotamian writings, in contrast with those in Genesis 12 onward, which have a more familiar historical tone. The fact that they follow ancient norms does not negate their inspired purpose. Theologian C. John Collins writes:

> These stories include divine action, symbolism, and imaginative elements; the purpose of the stories is to lay the foundation for a worldview, without being taken in a "literalistic" fashion. We should nevertheless see the story as having what we might call a *historical core*. . . . [So] if we abandon the conventional way of telling the Christian story, with its components of a good creation marred by the Fall, redemption as God's ongoing work to restore the creatures to their proper functioning . . . then we really give up all chance of understanding the world.[26]

The stories in Genesis 1–11 contain symbolism similar to other ancient Near Eastern stories. Understanding these symbols and norms helps us understand what God is saying through the story, while we avoid the trap of thinking its purpose is un-historical. Taking this approach frees us from getting stuck on unnecessary scientific questions in the Bible, such as *When was the exact year of the Creation?* Thus, if archaeology tells us Jericho was inhabited continually from 9,500 B.C. onward—more than a 6,000-year "literal" genealogy allows—we need not worry. We can be fascinated to learn more about the discovery and still honor God's Word.

CREATIVE LANGUAGE. This is an aspect of purpose that is often missed. We need to read the Bible with our senses connected to our heart. For example, what about powerful imagery? The Psalmist once wrote, "Your word is a lamp to my feet, and a light for my path" (Psalm 119:105). The vivid analogy of a lamp reminds us to let Scripture be our guide.

In the same way, we must appreciate the way a biblical author uses words to move us to action. Images, rhymes (in the original language), exaggerations, metaphor, and much more are used by the author to capture our imagination. We need to see and act on every intended word.

And how do we discover the vitality of these messages in Scripture? Eugene Peterson argues that a practice called *Lectio divina* is the best solution. As salt can "bring life to otherwise bland foods," he writes:

> *Lectio divina* provides us with a discipline . . . for recovering the context, restoring the intricate web of relationships to which the Scriptures give witness but that are so easily lost or obscured in the act of writing. [It has] four elements: *lectio* (we read the text), *meditatio* (we meditate the text), *oratio* (we pray the text), and *contemplatio* (we live the text).[27]

Of course, there are many other aspects of interpretation beyond the scope of this essay. I leave these as an exercise for you (the reader); it is worth our time to learn the details.

In summary, how do we discover the purpose of a Bible passage? We consider its audience, genre, form, and creative life. These guide our interpretation. Moreover, they help us to decide when a passage is making scientific or historical statements. And we have confidence because our interpretation is driven by the purpose of the text—by faithfulness to the words and the Word of God. True *fidelity* requires us to appreciate how the Scripture comes to life. So pursue the meaning of the text, and then take meaningful action. Reading the Bible should bring vitality and change to our lives. Otherwise, we are missing the point. God's Word is written so we may have life—and have it abundantly!

~

Your word is a lamp to my feet
and a light for my path.
Psalm 119:105

For discussion

1. What is something new that you learned in this essay?

2. How would you summarize the concept of *fidelity* as an aspect of Bible study?

3. In what ways does limited awareness of genre hinder our interpretation of the Bible ?

4. Proverbs 3:1–2 reads, *"Do not forget my teaching, but keep my commands in your heart, for they will prolong your life many years" (The Message)*. Do you think this is a fair motivation for interpreting the Bible accurately? Why or why not?

5. Bible scholars regularly study ancient texts in the cultures around Israel, such as law codes, treaties, epic myths, and histories. How do you think this can help us understand the Old Testament better?

6. We can change our mind about the meaning of Bible passages when we receive new information. What types of passages are more difficult to change our mind about?

7. Brainstorm some practical skills that Christians need in order to interpret difficult Bible passages.

8. How much time are you able to give to research when you need to make up your mind about a Bible passage? What would make this process easier for you?

9. What role do you think science should play, if any, in our study of Old Testament genealogies?

10. What are some ways you want to add life and vitality to your personal Bible reading?

[1] Image source: siarchives.si.edu / NMAH.

[2] See "Star-Spangled Banner and the War of 1812," *Encyclopedia Smithsonian*, at si.edu/Encyclopedia_SI/nmah/starflag.htm.

[3] John Stott, *Understanding the Bible*, 16.

[4] Henri Blocher, *In the Beginning*, 18.

[5] N. T. Wright, *The Last Word*, 73.

[6] Eugene Peterson, *Eat This Book*, 88.

[7] James Ussher, *Annals of the World*, 1.

[8] W. H. Green, "Primeval Chronology," *Bibliotheca Sacra* 47 (1890): 286–291. Also at biblicalstudies.org.uk/pdf/bsac/1890_285_green.pdf

[9] John Walton, *The NIV Application Commentary: Genesis*, 367–368. For example, "Jebusites" in Genesis 10:16 is a tribal name.

[10] The traditional Masoretic text lists nine generations in Genesis 11, but Luke 3:36 and the Septuagint text list ten generations.

[11] Bruce Waltke, *An Old Testament Theology*, 197. See also Kenneth Kitchen, *Ancient Orient and Old Testament*, 35–39; Walton, 283; and commentaries by Archer, Arnold, Cassuto, Hamilton, Kidner, Matthews, Sarna, Wenham, and Westermann.

[12] Gerhard Hasel, "Genesis 5 and 11: Chronogenealogies in the Biblical History of Beginnings," *Origins* 7, no. 1 (1980): 25. Also at grisda.org/origins-07023.

[13] RJS, "Genesis 4–5: Biblical Genealogies," Jesus Creed (blog), at patheos.com/blogs/jesuscreed/2009/04/14/genesis-4-5-biblical-genealogies-rjs.

[14] $1/(0.4^{20}) = 90,949,470$. But there are 210 combinations of four different digits, so $1/(210 \times 0.4^{20}) = 433,093$. Note that Genesis 5 also includes the formula *lived a total Z years and died*, but Z only summarizes X and Y and is not an independent number.

[15] Carol Hill, "Making Sense of the Numbers of Genesis," *Perspectives on Science and Christian Faith* 55, no. 4 (2003): 241. Also at asa3.org/ASA/PSCF/2003/PSCF12-03Hill.pdf.

[16] Genealogies in Mesopotamia are often lists of kings. See Walton, *Ancient Israelite Literature in its Cultural Context*, 127–131.

[17] See Jacob Klein, "The 'Bane' of Humanity: A Lifespan of One Hundred and Twenty Years," *Acta Sumerologica* 12 (1990): 62, 69. See also G. Kontopoulos, "Getting Old in Ancient Egypt," *ANE Today* VI, no 4, at asor.org/anetoday/2018/04/Getting-Old-In-Ancient+Egypt.

[18] Larry Pierce and Ken Ham, "Are There Gaps in the Genesis Genealogies?" in *The New Answers Book 2*, ed. Ken Ham, 175.

[19] The *Leningrad Codex* (Masoretic text) is scanned as Text #264 at seforimonline.org/seforimdb. Individual chapters can be viewed at commons.wikimedia.org/wiki/Category:Codex_Leningradensis. The passages of Genesis in Figure 7.4 and 7.5 are at 5:2:1–8, 10:1:25–10:2:2, and 56:1:5–8 (page:column:line).

[20] Note that את is used for definite direct objects only. It is not used for indefinite direct objects.

[21] Pierce and Ham, 177.

[22] In the Septuagint version of Exodus 12:40, Israel spent 430 years in Egypt and Canaan combined. Abraham's family was 215 years in Canaan, thus the Egyptian captivity was only 215 years. But since Septuagint genealogies are erratic (Methuselah died 17 years after the Flood), this solution is unlikely.

[23] See studylight.org/lex/heb/hwview.cgi?n=03205. Deuteronomy 4:25 is an example of the *hiphil* causative stem. Some critics misinterpret *hiphil*, e.g. Sarfati, "Biblical chronogenealogies," *Journal of Creation* 17, no. 3: 16, also at creation.com/journal-of-creation-tj-173.

[24] Gordon Fee and Douglas Stuart, *How to Read the Bible for All Its Worth*, 4th edition, 33–35.

[25] Hugh Ross, *The Genesis Question*, 108–110, and Sarfati, 17.

[26] C. John Collins, "Adam and Eve as Historical People, and Why It Matters," *Perspectives on Science and Christian Faith* 62, no. 3 (2010): 151, 161. Also at asa3.org/ASA/PSCF/2010/PSCF9-10dyn.html. Also Kenneth Kitchen, *On the Reliability of the Old Testament*, 447.

[27] Peterson, 90–91.

8

Optimism:
resolving our differences well

Think of a topic in science that generates a lot of heat. In particular, think of one that raises tough questions for followers of Jesus today. You can find a long list of scientific topics in the news on any given day. What about a topic that affects how you understand the Bible, Creation, or the person of God? How will you decide what is true on that topic and what is not?

All believers encounter controversial topics in science. After all, Christian theology is holistic—it informs our views about nearly every facet of life. We should expect to have lively discussions about ideas in biology, geology, astronomy, and many other fields of study. If you are like me, you probably have some unresolved questions about science and what they mean for your faith. Some notable questions that concern Christians today include:

Whether human DNA shows evidence of an original pair of ancestors—a question of origin;

whether Earth's features were formed over the last 4 billion years or over the last 6,000 years—a question of process;

whether humans are the primary cause of climate change over the past two centuries—a question of causation;

and whether the physical conditions of the universe are uniquely suited for life—a question of design.

These are very complex questions. But apart from their theological value, just answering the *scientific aspect* of these questions is not very simple. I once spent three summers doing research in a molecular physics laboratory.[1] I know it is not easy to design an experiment, even for smaller studies, and concisely explain the details to others. How then can the average person assess the results of a major scientific study on one of the topics above? You need a high level of familiarity with that science (and some patience to follow technical arguments) to make informed decisions about it.

Moreover, heated debates abound in the media today. There are soft voices, loud voices, majorities, and minorities for every big topic in science. And not everything you read is reliable. Do you want to know whether a statement is good science, pseudo-science, or just plain nuts? It will take time and effort to sort it out. Like me, you may struggle to maintain *optimism* about finding good answers in this remarkable sea of noise. You need wisdom and experience to discern between the voices.

Even if you tune out the noise, another problem remains: reliable voices sometimes differ from each other. On the four questions above, good people hold conflicting points of view. Why? Most often, it is because disagreements are essential to the scientific process, as one hypothesis is tested against another. But disagreements also arise any time related fields of study are involved. For example, who knows whether the conditions of the universe are uniquely suited for life? Astrobiologists? Mathematicians? Philosophers or theologians? Each discipline has its own approach to the question, so you need to weigh them carefully.

It is no surprise, then, that we have unresolved questions about science and our faith. Science and theology exist in a *relationship*, and disagreements are common in relationships. Without disagreements, in fact, we have no way to sort out the differences between points of view. Conflict (in the best sense of the word) is necessary to discover the truth on any given topic. Conflict leads to better understanding.

This reality leads us to a very important question. Does our posture in a conflict matter? If conflict is good, what if the *way* we go about it affects our ability to see what is true? To see the challenge of posture, let's look at four moments in the history of astronomy and then evaluate the outcomes:

(Please refer to primary sources on the next page.)

1) Galileo Galilei, during the debate about the solar system in the 17ᵗʰ century, wrote that science and theology exist without dispute in separate domains. Thus he believed the Bible should not be used as a textbook for astronomy. Galileo's observations of the night sky in 1609 helped confirm the Sun-centered (or *heliocentric*) model of the solar system first proposed by Copernicus. This caused quite a stir since the earth-centered (or *geocentric*) view had been held for over a thousand years and was taught by the Church in Rome. Against all opposition, Galileo

held to his view that God inspired the Scripture to teach about salvation, not about the details of the universe.

2) In contrast, some people in Galileo's time saw science and theology as potential enemies. As noted by the 19th century historian Andrew White, the Scripture was often quoted to oppose the new astronomy. For example, the theologian Fromundus challenged the idea that the earth orbits the sun by citing Psalm 19:5, in which the sun rises daily from the earth. As a result, the Church would deny the heliocentric view for another 200 years. White's famous *warfare thesis* is a common assumption about the relationship between Christianity and science.

3) Albert Einstein, in the first debates about the Big Bang, was too cautious toward the idea of God's involvement in the universe. As noted by astronomer Robert Jastrow, the initial evidence for an expanding universe startled scientists because they implied that the universe had a Beginning—a supernatural origin. This idea initially bothered Einstein so much that he added an extra constant to his theory of relativity, forcing it to predict an unchanging, eternal universe. As evidence for the Big Bang expansion grew in the 1920s, however, Einstein removed the extra constant. He later admitted it was the "biggest blunder he had made in his entire life."[6]

4) In reflection, young-earth astronomer Jason Lisle argues that scientists in Einstein's time were simply hostile to the idea of God's involvement in the universe (and even the existence of God). Looking back to the debates about the Big Bang, Lisle believes that scientists were blinded by naturalism, the idea that matter and nature are the

FAITH AND SCIENCE IN CONFLICT?

Galileo Galilei, in "Letter to the Grand Duchess" (1615):

> Since the Holy Ghost did not intend to teach us whether heaven moves or stands still, whether its shape is spherical or like a discus or extended in a plane, nor whether the earth is located at its center or off to one side, then so much the less was it intended to settle for us any other conclusion of the same kind. . . . Now if the Holy Spirit has purposely neglected to teach us propositions of this sort as irrelevant to the highest goal (that is, to our salvation), how can anyone affirm that it is obligatory to take sides on them, that one belief is required by faith, while the other side is erroneous? . . .
>
> I would say here something that was heard from an ecclesiastic of the most eminent degree: "That the intention of the Holy Ghost is to teach us how one goes to heaven, not how heaven goes."[2]

Andrew Dickson White, in *A History of the Warfare of Science with Theology in the History of Christendom* (1899):

> For the final assault upon [Galileo] a park of heavy artillery was at last wheeled into place. It may be seen on all the scientific battlefields. It consists of general denunciation; and in 1631 Father Melchior Inchofer, of the Jesuits, brought his artillery to bear upon Galileo with this declaration: "The opinion of the earth's motion is of all heresies the most abominable, the most pernicious, the most scandalous; the immovability of the earth is thrice sacred; argument against the immortality of the soul, the existence of God, and the incarnation, should be tolerated sooner than an argument to prove that the earth moves."
>
> From the other end of Europe came a powerful echo. From the shadow of the cathedral of Antwerp, the noted theologian Fromundus gave forth his famous treatise [declaring] that "sacred Scripture fights against the Copernicans." To prove that the sun revolves about the earth, he cites the passage in the Psalms which speaks of the sun "which cometh forth as a bridegroom out of his chamber."[3]

FAITH AND SCIENCE IN CONFLICT?   *continued*

Robert Jastrow, in *God and the Astronomers* (1978):

> Around this time, signs of irritation began to appear among the scientists. Einstein was the first to complain. He was disturbed by the idea of a Universe that blows up, because it implied that the world had a beginning. In a letter to de Sitter, discovered in a box of old records in Leiden some years ago, Einstein wrote "This circumstance [of an expanding Universe] irritates me," and in another letter about the expanding Universe, "To admit such possibilities seems senseless."

> This is curiously emotional language for a discussion of some mathematical formulas. I suppose that the idea of a beginning in time annoyed Einstein because of its theological implications. We know he had well-defined feelings about God, but not as the Creator or the Prime Mover. For Einstein, the existence of God was proved by the laws of nature; that is, the fact that there was order in the Universe and man could discover it.[4]

Jason Lisle, in *Taking Back Astronomy: The Heavens Declare Creation* (2006):

> I have found that most people who believe in billions of years also believe in the "big-bang theory." The big bang is a secular speculation about the origin of the universe; it is an alternative to the Bible. The big bang attempts to explain the origin of the universe without God. It can be considered the cosmic equivalent of particles–to–people evolution. Sadly, a lot of Christians have bought into the idea of the big bang, without realizing that it is based on the anti-biblical philosophy of naturalism (there is no God, nature is all there is or ever was).

> Furthermore, they are generally not aware that the big bang contradicts the Bible on a number of points and has many scientific problems as well.[5]

only things that exist. He concludes that astronomers speculated about the Big Bang because they needed an atheistic explanation for the origin of the universe.

These crucial moments in astronomy highlight a major challenge: a wrong posture toward the issues will cloud our thinking. Specifically, rigid assumptions or attitudes affect our ability to interpret the evidence in front of us.

Nowhere is this more clear than in the Galileo affair. Galileo assumed that studying nature was the best way to decide about the orbits of the planets. This forced him to ask, *What do I observe through the telescope?* And he saw, among other things, that Venus has phases that indicate it orbits the Sun. He concluded that heliocentrism is a better model of the solar system. In contrast, some scholars wary of the telescope only presumed to ask, *What does the Bible say?* And they concluded that the Sun and planets orbit a stationary Earth. A narrow assumption led to a wrong answer.

Overheated attitudes were also a major obstacle in the Galileo affair. For example, Galileo used one of his books to mock the Pope's traditional geocentric beliefs about the solar system.[7] This infuriated the Pope, who promptly put the famous scientist on trial. Galileo was condemned and ordered to renounce the earth's motion as heresy. And so, despite the powerful clarity of the new astronomy, the truth was buried in the midst of a polarizing debate.

Finally, Jason Lisle's skeptical view of modern scientists leads him astray. He assumes that astronomers were eager to embrace the Big Bang because it supported a godless view of the universe. Nothing is further from the truth. In actuality, atheists and agnostics *opposed* the theory because it weakened their mechanistic worldview. Arthur Eddington, the astronomer who famously confirmed Einstein's theory of relativity in 1919, openly resented the Big Bang:

> Philosophically, the notion of a beginning of the present order of nature is repugnant to me. . . . We are thus driven to admit anti-chance [i.e., a Designer or Creator], and apparently the best thing we can do with it is to sweep it up into a heap at the beginning of time.[8]

Likewise, astronomer Fred Hoyle (who coined the term *Big Bang*) called the theory a "distinctly unsatisfactory notion."[8] In fact, it took 40 years for most astronomers to concur that the universe had expanded from a single origin. This was no crutch for blinded scientists, and Lisle misses it completely.

When making decisions about what is true in nature, the real problem is not our lack of knowledge; nor is it the flood of misinformation. The problem is that we often begin conversations with a negative or oppositional posture. We may believe that scientific truth is objective, but the process of *finding* that truth is often very subjective.

Faith and science in relationship

Rigid attitudes and assumptions have the power to prevent us from seeing valid ideas in science. Subtly, we may oppose an idea without realizing we do not see its nuances. After all, theologians in Rome were as devout as Galileo and yet they arrived at an opposite conclusion about the solar system. Virtue and skill make no difference—we are blind to truth-critical nuances unless we adjust our posture.

Consequently, I want to ask two questions that will help us hold a useful stance whenever we study a topic in science. (1) *How do theology and science relate to each other?* We need to know how their domains overlap. And (2) *How do we improve our ability to discern truth in science?* We need tools and skills to navigate our unresolved questions.

First of all, what is the relationship between science and theology? To say it another way, what are their domains of knowledge and authority? It turns out there are many ways to look at this relationship. Here are three possible models, which I have adapted from scientist Richard Bube.

CONFLICT (OR CONCORD)

The conflict model says, "Science and theology tell us the *same* kinds of things about the *same* things."[9] They share the same domain. Therefore, when scientific and theological claims contradict, one is right, and the other is wrong:

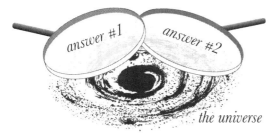

theology *vs* science   Fig. 8.1

For example, this model assumes that astronomy and the Bible make direct claims about the age of the universe. Thus if science is right, we must reinterpret Scripture to align with modern astronomy. But if the Bible is right, then the science is wrong and needs to be corrected. No surprise here: *conflict* (or warfare) is the default mode for many people. This is especially true for those who interpret Scripture in a highly literal way (the Bible always wins) and for scientists who promote naturalism or atheism (science always wins).

Of course, full rejection is not the only option here. Some

Christians avoid the warfare mindset because they believe the Bible already agrees with modern science. For example, what if Genesis 1:1 describes the Big Bang? This option is called *concord* (i.e., agreement) instead of *conflict*. But regardless of the distinction, the model is the same: theology and science speak about the same domain in the same ways.

COMPARTMENTAL

The compartmental model says, "Science and theology tell us *different* kinds of things about *different* things."[9] Conflict is impossible in this situation because scientific and theological statements have no common ground:

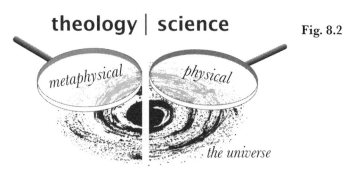

theology | science   Fig. 8.2

metaphysical   *physical*

the universe

For example, if science tells us about the age of the universe, then the Bible tells us about morality and spirituality. A distinction is drawn between physical and metaphysical realities, which are now seen as separate domains. Galileo advocated for this model, as we saw earlier. It is also called "nonoverlapping magisteria" (or *NOMA*) by secular biologist Stephen Jay Gould, who wrote:

> These two magisteria [i.e., domains of authority] do not overlap. . . . To cite the old clichés, science gets the ages of rocks, and religion the rock of ages; science studies how the heavens go, religion how to go to heaven.[10]

COMPLEMENTARY

The complementary model says, "Science and theology tell us *different* kinds of things about the *same* things."[9] When they stay within their limits, scientific and theological statements work in harmony to describe the same reality:

Fig. 8.3

theology +science

the universe

In this model, science studies the physical reasons for things in nature—what are called *immediate causes*. Whereas theology describes the deeper reasons behind these things—what are called *ultimate causes*. Thus, if science tells us how the stars and planets formed, then theology teaches us how and why God guides each process toward his purpose. We need both insights to have a complete picture of reality. Theologian John Walton describes this with a "layer-cake" analogy because the idea of divine purpose adds a layer to our scientific understanding without introducing conflict: "The mechanisms [God] used to bring the material cosmos into existence are of little consequence as long as they are seen as the tools in his hands."[11]

Which of these three models is better at describing the relationship of theology and science? As attractive as they are, each model does have a weakness—our reality does not fit cleanly into these categories! Here are three examples:

1. The Bible does not answer most physical questions about nature. It often appears complementary. Nonetheless, it does make some surprising claims that directly conflict with science, such as about the resurrection of Jesus.
2. Likewise, science does not answer most moral questions. But science increasingly gives insight into things that were once the exclusive realm of religion or philosophy, such as the motivation and nature of love.
3. Other times, theology and science are purely complementary. Psalm 139:13 says that God "knit me together in my mother's womb," which is a purposeful statement that only *enriches* our scientific understanding of pregnancy.

How do theology and science relate to each other, then? Our answer needs to capture the complexity of overlap between these two ways of knowing. So I find it helpful to describe a fourth model of relationship.

COINHERENT

The coinherent model says, "Science and theology tell us *many* kinds of things about the *same* things in the universe, by working together in different ways." I have adapted this concept from theologian-scientist Ross Hastings. The word *coinherent* describes an interdependent relationship in which each discipline is "inherent" or essential to the other.

In practice, coinherence is not a rigid model. It is a way to describe the nuances of theology and science when they are complementary at times but in other times they fit a conflict/concord model. They enrich each other in various ways. Thus theology often operates in the same *domain* as science (the created universe), but not consistently in the same *way* each time, as illustrated in Figure 8.4:

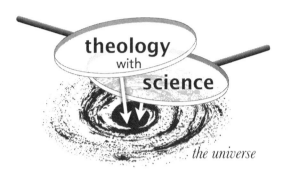

Fig. 8.4

the universe

From a Christian point of view, all of Creation finds its source in Jesus Christ, "in whom all things hold together" (Colossians 1:17). Therefore, science and theology uncover the same ultimate Truth. But since they have different ways of knowing that truth, scientific and theological statements operate with unique voices *alongside* each other on any topic. Ross Hastings clarifies:

> A proposal of coinherence between theology and science is not a "mixing" of the disciplines, just as the human and Divine natures of the incarnate Christ are not confused or mixed. Each has its own irreducibly distinct entity as a discipline. . . . [Coinherence] simply asserts that there is a place for each discipline in the other.[12]

This brings us to the second question we asked earlier: How do we improve our ability to discern truth in science? Could the model of *coinherence* help Christians hold a better posture in a scientific debate? Absolutely! If theology and science are coinherent, then we will keep an open dialogue between these two ways of knowing. Openness ensures that all truths will be heard, even in the midst of disagreement.

I believe this posture toward open conversation is best described as an attitude of *optimism*.

Clarity through optimism

Perhaps a different attitude could help us with tough science and theology questions, such as civility or kindness or mutual respect. But optimism is far better. Optimism is a positive outlook that bears fruit in any relationship. It *facilitates* civility. It *fosters* kindness and respect. Optimism is the soothing ointment that keeps people talking even in the midst of a conflict. And therefore, it helps us see the nuances of truth around us more clearly.

Theology and science have a clear mutual interest in the natural world (even as theology extends beyond it). And as we say earlier, their truth statements overlap in various ways, depending on the topic. This means we have work to do! I want to suggest two ways that the practice of *optimism* will help us find clarity in our search for truth.

First of all, hold a positive attitude toward anyone who is knowledgeable about a scientific or biblical topic. I do not believe we must turn a blind eye toward their motivations or level of skill, of course. But optimism motivates us to trust that there is something to learn in each conversation. After all, most of us are not likely to dive into a geology paper or learn the technical skills of a geneticist. This places all of us—every person on Earth—into a situation where we rely on others for insight. Consider these words from Michael Polanyi, the 20th century philosopher of science:

> The amount of knowledge which we can justify from evidence directly available to us can never be large. The overwhelming proportion of our factual beliefs continue therefore to be held at second hand through trusting others, and in the great majority of cases our trust is placed in the authority of comparatively few people of widely acknowledged standing.[13]

In a modern community, we trust others to mediate the knowledge we lack—whether in physics, medicine, history, languages, or even biblical culture. At the same time, we also need to evaluate and carefully integrate the things we learn. Discernment matters. So what is the best way to retain an open *and discerning* posture toward others? I suggest we do what scientists and theologians have always done: create habits that limit the influence of ideology and false information on our work. Here are some starting points:

(1) Work at separating content from personal beliefs. The facts often speak for themselves, regardless of a researcher's agenda. It is possible to learn astronomy from a Christian, a Hindu, or an atheist, and major discoveries are made by people of every background. (2) Seek to balance opinions from respectable people. Reading the footnotes in a book, paper, or web article is a valuable way to discover who the important voices are on a topic. Do not trust researchers who are unable to articulate opposing viewpoints and leave no references. (3) Even better, pursue people who display an open-minded engagement with all forms of knowledge. It is better to trust researchers who study broadly and draw conclusions slowly. They are valuable sources, likely to deal with the information accurately. (4) Recognize when a researcher is far outside their level of experience. Wisdom grows with time and training. And (5) remember that faith and science have no inherent conflict. Historically, the battle is often between naturalism and theism, which take opposing views of God, but not with science itself. Some scientists have even converted to Christianity *because* of discoveries in astronomy or evolutionary biology. Science is a powerful tool, not a belief in itself.

Fig. 8.5 "Galileo shows the satellites of Jupiter to the senators of Venice" (1876), by Louis Figuier. This engraving captures the remarkable fascination that people took in Galileo's discoveries.[15]

And second, we should keep a positive mindset toward scientific information in an age of noisy and fast-paced commentary. I am not suggesting that we accept all information blindly, of course. That would be a very poor idea! But optimism calls us to trust that real truth is out there—in articles, books, research papers, university classes, and even in the news. We simply need good ways to identify trustworthy sources and curate the information we find.

How do we do this? In the flood of media today, we cannot verify every last bit and byte. (Nor can we do this with conventional literature). This is an increasing reality in the modern world. But we can defend ourselves from various forms of *disinformation* as we seek out the truth. Therefore, in the digital age it is our job to assess the *reputational path* of the information we find, and to study the motivations of its providers.[14] Here are some starting points:

(1) Steer away from poorly-sourced material. Expediency is the enemy of truth in scientific writing. Someone who makes dramatic, unsupported points on many topics is unreliable. (2) Whenever possible, follow references and see if they are quoted accurately. This is a sign of a careful presenter. (3) Use the tools at your disposal—the scientific method and biblical interpretation—to evaluate what you read. Gut reactions are likely to lead you astray. (4) Avoid rapid-cycle media. Scientific reflections that take years are much better than those made in the heat of a debate. And (5) Cultivate a library of trusted sources. Continue to expand your understanding throughout your life. In other words, build that bookshelf!

Optimism enables us to learn from others despite our differences. In this way we can learn from Galileo, whose approach to science was truly infectious. Despite his many weaknesses, his work still enabled others to search the stars (Figure 8.5), write equations, and learn about the cosmos. We can adopt this attitude. Let us engage in science with the same optimism and care. All truth comes from God— so let us resolve our differences well.

~

Show me your ways, Lord,
Teach me your paths.
Psalm 25:4

For discussion

1. What is something new that you learned in this essay?

2. What thoughts or feelings do you experience when you are discussing a heated science topic with others?

3. *"Let every good and true Christian understand that wherever truth may be found, it belongs to his Master"* (Saint Augustine).[16] Do you think this is a useful starting point for Christians thinking about science and theology?

4. Which model of relationship between science and theology do you identify with the most? Why?

5. Do you think climate change should be categorized as a *theological, biblical,* or *scientific* topic? How so?

6. What skills would you add to those discussed in the essay for discerning reliable sources of information?

7. Are the skills discussed in this essay transferrable to other conversations or areas of life? If so, give some examples.

8. What are some ways to distinguish between high- and low-quality arguments when hearing others' opinions about a topic in science?

9. Traditional Christians have various positions about the age of the universe, God's method of creating the world, biological evolution, the prevalence of miracles, and so on. What core values should Christians keep when they have conversations on these topics?

10. How would a posture of optimism help you to improve your own learning and help others?

[1] At the Pacific Northwest National Laboratory, I conducted the laboratory research for "Electron beam effects on $(CH_2)_{17}$ self-assembled monolayer SiO–Si specimens," *Journal of Vacuum Science Technology A* 12 (1994). Also at doi.org/10.1116/1.579197.

[2] Galileo Galilei, "Letter to the Grand Duchess Christina," quoted in Stillman Drake, *Discoveries and Opinions of Galileo*, 185–186.

[3] Andrew Dickson White, *A History of the Warfare of Science with Theology in the History of Christendom*, 139.

[4] Robert Jastrow, *God and the Astronomers*, 20–21.

[5] Jason Lisle, *Taking Back Astronomy: The Heavens Declare Creation*, 43.

[6] George Gamow, "The Evolutionary Universe," *Scientific American* 195, no. 3 (1956): 140.

[7] Galileo, *Dialogue Concerning the Two Chief World Systems*; in *Opere* VII, 33. Galileo used a character called Simplicio (i.e., simpleton) to mimic the Pope's beliefs. See Dan Guenther, "The Galileo Affair Revisited," Regent College (May 2010), 9, at academia.edu/33151519.

[8] Arthur S. Eddington, "The End of the World," *Nature* 127, no. 3203: 450 and 452; and Fred Hoyle, *The Nature of the Universe*, 124.

[9] Richard Bube, *Putting it All Together*, 55+75, 95, and 167, respectively.

[10] Stephen Jay Gould, *Rocks of Ages*, 6.

[11] John Walton, *The Lost World of Genesis One*, 117. See also *teleology*.

[12] Ross Hastings, *Echoes of Coinherence*, 5.

[13] Michael Polanyi, *Personal Knowledge*, 208.

[14] Gloria Origgi, "Say goodbye to the information age," *Aeon*, 14 Mar. 2018, at aeon.co/ideas/say-goodbye-to-the-information-age-its-all-about-reputation-now. See also Del Ratzsche, *Science and its Limits*, 162, regarding the need to speak truth with accuracy.

[15] Engraving in Louis Figuier, *Lives of Illustrious Scholars* (1876), page facing 112. Image source: gallica.bnf.fr / BnF.

[16] Saint Augustine, *On Christian Doctrine*, 2.18.

Doxology

Praise him, sun and moon;
Praise him, all you shining stars.
Praise him, you highest heavens
and you waters above the skies.

Let them praise the name of the Lord,
for at his command they were created.

Psalm 148:3–5

———

To conclude, therefore, let nobody out of a vain sense
of sobriety or ill-applied moderation think or maintain
that a person can search too far, or be too well-studied,
in the book of God's Word; or in the book
of God's Works, divinity or philosophy;

But rather let all people endeavour an
endless progress or proficiency in both.

Sir Francis Bacon

Works cited

Letter to the reader

Ferngren, Gary B. *Science and Religion: A Historical Introduction*. Baltimore: Johns Hopkins University Press, 2002.

Gundry, Stanley. Counterpoints: Bible and Theology (series). Grand Rapids: Zondervan.

Haarsma, Deborah, and Loren Haarsma. *Origins: Christian Perspectives on Creation, Evolution, and Intelligent Design*. Grand Rapids: Faith Alive Christian Resources, 2011.

Stump, J. B. *Science and Christianity: An Introduction to the Issues.* Hoboken: Wiley & Sons, 2016.

1 Suspense

Augustine of Hippo. *The Literal Meaning of Genesis*. Translated by John Hammond Taylor. Vol. 41 of *Ancient Christian Writers*, edited by Johannes Quasten, Walter J. Burghardt, and Thomas Comerford Lawler. New York: Newman Press, 1982. Also at doi.org/10.2307/2850007.

_____. *The City of God*. Translated by Marcus Dods. In vol. 2 of *Nicene and Post-Nicene Fathers of the Christian Church, 1st Series*, edited by Philip Schaff. 1887. Reprint, Grand Rapids: Eerdmans, 1988. Also at ccel.org/ccel/schaff/npnf102, translated by Philip Schaff.

Calvin, John. *Commentary on the Book of Psalms*, vol. 4. Translated by James Anderson. 1847. Reprint, Grand Rapids: Baker, 1981. Also at ccel.org/ccel/calvin/calcom11.

Flammarion, Camille. *The Atmosphere: Popular Meteorology*. Paris: Hachette, 1888. Also at gallica.bnf.fr/ark:/12148/bpt6k408619m (French).

Guenther, D. E. "Reconciling the Faith: Christian Students Who Move from Fear to Engagement the Sciences." In *Proceedings of the Inaugural Faith & Science Conference*, edited by David R. Bundrick and Steve Badger, 325–334. Springfield: Gospel Publishing House, 2011. Also as paper submitted to Regent College, July 2009, at academia.edu/33151748.

Holy Office of the Inquisition. "Sentence (22 June 1633)." Quoted in *The Galileo Affair: A Documentary History*, edited and translated by Maurice A. Finocchiaro. Berkeley: University of California Press, 1989. Also at creating history.com/galileo-galileis-sentence-22-june-1633.

Irenaeus. *Against Heresies*. Translated by Cleveland Coxe. In *The Apostolic Fathers: with Justin Martyr and Irenaeus*, vol. 1 of *The Ante-Nicene Fathers*, edited by Alexander Roberts and James Donaldson. 1867. Reprint, Grand Rapids: Eerdmans, 1979. Also at ccel.org/ccel/schaff/anf01, translated by Philip Schaff.

Luther, Martin. *Lectures on Genesis*. Translated by George V. Shick. In vol. 1 of *Luther's Works*, edited by Jaroslav Pelikan. St. Louis: Concordia Publishing House, 1958. Also at archive.org/details/werkekritischege 42luthuoft (German).

———. *Table Talk*. Translated by Theodore G. Tappert. Vol. 54 of *Luther's Works*, edited by Helmut T. Lehmann. Philadelphia: Fortress Press, 1967. Also at archive.org/details/werketischreden10204 luthuoft (German).

Meldenius, Rupertus. *An Exhortation for Peace at the Church of the Augsburg Confession of Theologians*. In *History of the Reformation: 1517–1648*, 650–653, vol. 7 of *History of the Christian Church*, edited and translated by Philip Schaff. Grand Rapids: Eerdmans, 1910. Also at ccel.org/s/schaff/hcc7.

Morris, Henry M. *Science and the Bible*. Revised edition. Chicago: Moody Press, 1986.

Scofield, Cyrus. *The Scofield Reference Bible*. New York: Oxford University Press, 1917. Also at studylight.org/com/srn.

"The Apostles' Creed." Quoted in *The Greek and Latin Creeds with Trans-*

lations, vol. 2 of *The Creeds of Christendom with a History and Critical Notes*, edited and translated by Philip Schaff. 1887. Reprint, New York: Harper & Brothers, 1919. Also at ccel.org/ccel/schaff/creeds2.

2 Delight

Bouma-Prediger, Stephen. *For the Beauty of the Earth: A Christian Vision for Creation Care*. 2nd edition. Grand Rapids: Baker Academic, 2010.

Dillard, Annie. *Pilgrim at Tinker Creek*. 1974. Reprint, New York: Harper Collins, 2007.

Drake, Stillman. *Galileo at Work: His Scientific Biography*. 1978. Reprint, Mineola: Dover Publications, 1995.

Encyclopædia Britannica. Chicago: Encyclopædia Britannica, 2010. Also at brittanica.com.

Foster, Michael. "The Christian Doctrine of Creation and the Rise of Modern Science." *Mind* 43, no. 172 (1934): 446–468. Also at doi.org/10.1093/mind/XLIII.172.446.

Francis of Assisi. "The Canticle of Brother Sun." Quoted in *Francis and Clare: The Complete Works*, edited and translated by Regis J. Armstrong and Ignatius C. Brady, 37–39. New York: Paulist Press, 1982. Also at ccel.org/ccel/schaff/hcc5, translated by Philip Schaff.

Galilei, Galileo. Letter to Kepler (19 August 1610). Translated by Dennis Danielson, personal correspondence, 2014.

Galilei, Galileo. *The Works of Galileo Galilei, National Edition*. Edited by Antonio Favaro. Florence: Giunti-Barbèra, 1934. Also at portalegalileo.museogalileo.it (Italian).

Huff, Toby E. *The Rise of Early Modern Science*. 3rd edition. Cambridge: Cambridge University Press, 2017.

Jaki, Stanley. *The Savior of Science.* Grand Rapids: Eerdmans, 2000.

Michelangelo. "The Creation of Adam." In the Sistine Chapel. Depicted in en.wikipedia.org/wiki/The_Creation_of_Adam.

Opere (Le Opere di Galileo Galilei). See Galilei, Galileo, *The Works of Galileo Galilei, National Edition*.

Plato. "Allegory of the Cave," in *The Republic*, VII. Translated by Benjamin Jowett. *Project Gutenberg*, 2008. At gutenberg.org/files/1497/1497-h/1497-h.htm.

Schaeffer, Francis A. *Pollution and the Death of Man: the Christian View of Ecology*. Wheaton: Tyndale House Publishers, 1970.

Schreiner, Susan. *The Theater of His Glory: Nature and the Natural Order in the Thought of John Calvin*. Grand Rapids: Baker Academic, 1991.

White, Lynn Jr.. "The Historical Roots of our Ecological Crisis." *Science* 10 March 1967, no. 155: 1202–1207. Also at doi.org/10.1126/science. 155.3767.1203 and asa3.org/ASA/PSCF/1969/JASA6-69White.html.

Wilson, E. O. *The Creation: An Appeal to Save Life on Earth*. New York: W. W. Norton, 2007.

3 Equity

Augustine of Hippo. *Expositions on the Book of Psalms*. In *Enarrationes In Psalmos 001-079, Patrologia Latina* 36, 518. Translated by Dennis Danielson, personal correspondence, 2014. Also at documenta catholicaomnia.eu (Latin).

_____. *On Christian Doctrine*. Translated by Marcus Dods. In vol. 2 of *Nicene and Post-Nicene Fathers of the Christian Church, 1st Series*, edited by Philip Schaff. 1887. Reprint, Grand Rapids: Eerdmans, 1988. Also at ccel.org/ccel/schaff/npnf102, translated by Philip Schaff.

Dawkins, Richard. *The God Delusion*. New York: Houghton Mifflin, 2006.

Galilei, Galileo. "Letter to the Grand Duchess Christina." Quoted in *Discoveries and Opinions of Galileo*, edited and translated by Stillman Drake, 173–216. New York: Anchor-Doubleday, 1957.

_____. *The Works of Galileo Galilei, National Edition*. Edited by Antonio Favaro. Florence: Giunti-Barbèra, 1934. Also at portalegalileo. museogalileo.it (Italian).

Morris, Henry, and John Whitcomb, *The Genesis Flood: the Biblical Record and its Scientific Implications*. Phillipsburg: Presbyterian and Reformed Press, 1961.

Murphy, George. "Reading God's Two Books." *Perspectives on Science and Christian Faith* 58, no. 1 (2006): 64–67. Also at asa3.org/ASA/PSCF/ 2006/PSCF3-06dyn.html.

Opere (*Le Opere di Galileo Galilei*). See Galilei, Galileo, *The Works of Galileo Galilei, National Edition*.

Ross, Hugh. *More Than a Theory: Revealing a Testable Model for Creation*. Grand Rapids: Baker Books, 2009.

Sproul, R. C. *Scripture Alone: The Evangelical Doctrine*. Phillipsburg: Presbyterian and Reformed Press, 2005.

Tanzella-Nitti, Giuseppe. "The Two Books Prior to the Scientific Revolution." *Perspectives on Science and Christian Faith* 57, no. 3 (2005): 235–248. Also at asa3.org/ASA/PSCF/2005/PSCF9-05dyn.html.

Van Till, Howard, Davis A. Young, and Clarence Menninga. *Science Held Hostage: What's Wrong With Creation Science AND Evolutionism*. Downer's Grove: Intervarsity Press, 1988.

Wise, Kurt. "Geology," in *In Six Days: Why Fifty Scientists Choose to Believe in Creation*, ed. J. Ashton, 351–355. Green Forest: Master Books, 2001.

4 Curiosity

Agassiz, Louis. *Methods of Study in Natural History*. Boston: Ticknor and Fields, 1863. Also at archive.org/details/methodsofstudyin1869agas.

Bacon, Francis. *A New Instrument of Science (Novum Organum)*. England, 1620. Reprint, New York: P. F. Collier & Son, 1902. Also at gutenberg.org/files/45988/45988-h/45988-h.htm.

Bowman, Sheridan. *Radiocarbon Dating*. Berkeley: University of California Press, 1990.

Copernicus, Nicolaus. *On the Revolutions of the Heavenly Spheres*. Portions quoted in *The Book of the Cosmos*, edited and translated by Dennis Danielson, 104–117. Cambridge: Perseus Publishing, 2000.

Cutler, Alan. *The Seashell on the Mountaintop*. New York: Plume, 2004.

Feynman, Richard. "The Pleasure of Finding Things Out," on BBC *Horizon*, 23 November 1981. Quoted in *The Pleasure of Finding Things Out: The Best Short Works of Richard P. Feynman*, edited by Michelle Feynman and Carl Feynman, 1–26. Cambridge: Basic Books, 1999.

————. *The Meaning of it All: Thoughts of a Citizen Scientist*. Edited by Jeffrey Robbins. New York: Basic Books, 1999.

Ham, Ken. "Searching For the 'Magic Bullet'." *Creation* 25, no. 2 (2003): 34–37. Also at creation.com/searching-for-the-magic-bullet.

Keith, M. L., and G. M. Anderson. "Radiocarbon Dating: Fictitious Results with Mollusk Shells." *Science*, 16 August 1963: 634–637. Also at sciencemag.org/content/141/3581/634.

Kepler, Johannes. "Letter to Hans Herwart." Quoted in Arthur Koestler, *The Sleepwalkers: A History of Man's Changing Vision of the Universe*, 345. 1959. Reprint, New York: Penguin Arkana, 1990.

Lister, Martin. *History of the Creatures of England*. London: J. Martyn, 1678. Also at catalog.lindahall.org/permalink/01lindahall_inst/1nrd31s/alma99537293405961.

Polanyi, Michael. *Personal Knowledge: Towards a Post-Critical Philosophy*. Chicago: University of Chicago Press, 1958.

Polkinghorne, John. *Quantum Physics and Theology: an Unexpected Kinship*. New Haven: Yale University Press, 2007.

Rockwell, David. *Exploring Glacier National Park*. Guilford: Falcon, 2002.

Rudwick, Martin J. S. *Earth's Deep History: How It Was Discovered and Why It Matters*. Chicago: The University of Chicago Press, 2014.

Steno, Nicolaus. *Elemental Specimens of Myology*. Amsterdam, 1669. Also at digitale.beic.it/BEIC:RD01:39bei_digitool4715289 (Latin).

Wright, N. T. *The New Testament and the People of God*. Minneapolis: Fortress Press, 1992.

5 Reverence

Arnold, Bill, and Brent Strawn. *The World Around the Old Testament: The People and Places of the Ancient Near East*. Grand Rapids: Baker Academic, 2016.

Augustine of Hippo. *The Literal Meaning of Genesis*. Translated by John Hammond Taylor. Vol. 41 of *Ancient Christian Writers*, edited by Johannes Quasten, Walter J. Burghardt, and Thomas Comerford Lawler. New York: Newman Press, 1982. Also at doi.org/10.2307/2850007.

Barrett, Michael, and Ardel B. Caneday, eds. *Four Views on the Historical Adam*. Grand Rapids: Zondervan, 2013.

Brown, F., S. Driver, and C. Briggs. *Hebrew and English Lexicon*. Oxford: Clarendon Press, 1936. Also at en.wikisource.org/wiki/Index:A_Hebrew_and_English_Lexicon_(Brown-Driver-Briggs).djvu.

Budge, E. A. Wallis. *The Gods of the Egyptians: or Studies in Egyptian Mythology*, vol. 2. New York: Dover Publications, 1969. Reprint, 1904.

Calvin, John. *Commentaries on the First Book of Moses Called Genesis*, vol 1. Translated by John King. Grand Rapids: Eerdmans, 1948. Also at ccel.org/ccel/calvin/calcom01.

_____. *Institutes of the Christian Religion*. Translated by Henry Beveridge. Edinburgh: Calvin Translation Society, 1845. Also at ccel.org/ccel/calvin/institutes.

Lisle, Jason. "The Expanding Universe," in *The New Answers Book 2*, 48–49, edited by Ken Ham. Green Forest: Master Books, 2008.

Mazzio, Carla. "Shakespeare and Science, c. 1600." *South Central Review* 26, no. 1 (2009): 1–23. Also at doi.org/10.1353/scr.0.0044.

Morris, Henry. "The Bible is a Textbook of Science." *Biblioteca Sacra* 121 (Fall 1964): 341–350. Also at icr.org/home/resources/resources_tracts_tbiatos.

Packer, J. I. *God Has Spoken: Revelation and the Bible*. 3rd edition. Grand Rapids: Baker Academic, 1994.

Ross, Hugh. *The Genesis Question: Scientific Advances and the Accuracy of Genesis*. 2nd edition. Colorado Springs: NavPress, 2001.

Schedl, Claus. *The Ancient Orient and Ancient Biblical History*. In vol. 1 of *History of the Old Testament*. New York: Alba House, 1973.

"The Chicago Statement on Biblical Inerrancy." Dallas Theological Seminary. At library.dts.edu/Pages/TL/Special/ICBI_1.pdf.

Walton, John. *The Lost World of Genesis One: Ancient Cosmology and the Origins Debate*. Downer's Grove: Intervarsity Press, 2009.

Wilberforce, William. *A Letter on the Abolition of the Slave Trade*. London: Luke Hansard & Sons, 1807. Also at archive.org/details/aletteronabolit00wilbgoog.

6 Focus

Alley, Richard B. "Concerning the Deposition and Diagenesis of Strata in Polar Firn." *Journal of Glaciology* 34 (1988): 283–90. Also at doi.org/10.3189/S0022143000007024.

_____. *The Two Mile Time Machine: Ice Cores, Abrupt Climate Change, and Our Future*. Princeton: Princeton University Press, 2000.

Alley, Richard, and Sridhar Anandkrishnan. "Variations in melt-layer
    frequency in the GISP2 ice core: implications for Holocene summer
    temperatures in central Greenland." *Annals of Glaciology* 21 (1995):
    64–70. Also at igsoc.org/annals.old/21.

Alley, Richard, and others. "Visual-stratigraphic dating of the GISP2 ice
    core: Basis, reproducibility, and application." *Journal of Geophysical
    Research* 102, no. C12 (1997): 26,378–26,381. Also at doi.org/
    10.1029/ 96JC03837.

Basil of Caesarea. "The Creation of the Heavens and the Earth."
    Translated by Agnes Clare Way. In *Saint Basil: Exegetical Homilies,* vol.
    46 of *The Fathers of the Church,* edited by Roy Joseph Deferrari.
    Washington, DC: The Catholic University of America Press, 1963.
    Also at archive.org/details/fathersofthechur013929mbp.

Clausen, Henrik, and others. "A comparison of the volcanic records
    over the past 4000 years from the Greenland Ice Core Project and
    Dye 3 Greenland ice cores." *Journal of Geophysical Research* 102, no.
    C12 (1997): 26,707–26,723. Also at doi.org/10.1029/97JC00587.

Guenther, D. E. "The Accommodation Doctrine." Paper submitted to
    Regent College, June 2010. At academia.edu/33151691.

Hutton, James. *Theory of the Earth, with Proofs & Illustrations.* 4 volumes.
    Edinburgh, 1795. Also at gutenberg.org/ebooks/12861.

Lewis, C. S. *The Discarded Image: An Introduction to Medieval and Renaissance
    Literature.* 1964. Reprint, Cambridge: Cambridge Univ. Press, 2000.

McMullin, Ernan. "Values in Science." *Zygon* 47, no. 4 (2012): 686–709.
    At doi.org/10.1111/j.1467-9744.2012.01298.x.

Meese, Debra, and others. "The Greenland Ice Sheet Project 2 depth-
    age scale: Methods and results." *Journal of Geophysical Research* 102, no.
    C12 (1997): 26,411–26,423. Also at doi.org/10.1029/ 97JC00269.

Morris, Henry, and John Whitcomb, *The Genesis Flood: the Biblical Record
    and its Scientific Implications.* Phillipsburg: Presbyterian and Reformed
    Press, 1961.

Oard, Michael. "Do Greenland ice cores show over one hundred
    thousand years of annual layers?" *Journal of Creation* 15, no. 3 (2001):
    39–42. Also at creation.com/journal-of-creation-tj-153.

_____. "Ice Cores vs. the Flood." *Journal of Creation* 18, no. 2 (2004):
    58–61. Also at creation.com/journal-of-creation-tj-182.

Popper, Karl. *The Logic of Scientific Discovery*. 1959. Reprint, New York: Routledge, 2008.

Ratzsch, Del. *Science & Its Limits*. 2nd edition. Downers Grove: InterVarsity Press, 2000.

Seely, Paul. "The GISP2 Ice Core: Ultimate Proof that Noah's Flood Was Not Global." *Perspectives on Science and Christian Faith* 55, no. 5 (2003): 252–260. Also at asa3.org/ASA/PSCF/2003/PSCF12-03dyn.html.

Van Till, Howard, Robert E. Snow, John H. Stek, and Davis A. Young. *Portraits of Creation: Biblical and Scientific Perspectives on the World's Formation*. Grand Rapids: Eerdman's, 1990.

Van Till, Howard, Davis A. Young, and Clarence Menninga. *Science Held Hostage: What's Wrong With Creation Science AND Evolutionism*. Downer's Grove: Intervarsity Press, 1988.

Vardiman, Larry. "Ice Cores and the Age of the Earth." *Acts & Facts* 21, no. 4. 01 April 1992. At icr.org/article/ice-cores-age-earth.

_____. *Ice Cores and the Age of the Earth*. El Cajon: Institute for Creation Research, 1993.

7 Fidelity

Blocher, Henri. *In the Beginning: The Opening Chapters of Genesis*. Downers Grove: InterVarsity Press, 1984.

Collins, C. John. "Adam and Eve as Historical People, and Why It Matters." *Perspectives on Science and Christian Faith* 62, no. 3 (2010): 147–165. Also at asa3.org/ASA/PSCF/2010/PSCF9-10dyn.html.

Fee, Gordon, and Douglas Stuart. *How to Read the Bible for All Its Worth: A Guide to Understanding the Bible*. 4th ed. Grand Rapids: Zondervan: 2014.

Green, William Henry. "Primeval Chronology." *Bibliotheca Sacra* 47 (1890): 285–303. Also at biblicalstudies.org.uk/pdf/bsac/1890_285_green.pdf.

Hasel, Gerhard. "Genesis 5 and 11: Chronogenealogies in the Biblical History of Beginnings." *Origins* 7, no. 1 (1980), 23–37. Also at grisda.org/origins-07023.

Hill, Carol. "Making Sense of the Numbers of Genesis." *Perspectives on Science and Christian Faith* 55, no. 4 (2003): 241. Also at asa3.org/ASA/PSCF/2003/PSCF12-03Hill.pdf.

Kitchen, Kenneth. *Ancient Orient and Old Testament*. Downers Grove: InterVarsity, 1975.

_____. *On the Reliability of the Old Testament*. Grand Rapids: Eerdmans, 2003.

Klein, Jacob. "The 'Bane' of Humanity: A Lifespan of One Hundred and Twenty Years." *Acta Sumerologica* 12 (1990): 57–70. Also at academia.edu/17113185/The_Bane_of_Humanity_A_Lifespan_of_One_Hundred_Twenty_Years_Acta_Sumerologica_12_1990_.

Kontopoulos, Grigorios I. "Getting Old in Ancient Egypt." *The Ancient Near East Today* VI, no. 4 (2018). At www.asor.org/anetoday/2018/04/Getting-Old-In-Ancient+Egypt.

Peterson, Eugene. *Eat This Book: A Conversation in the Art of Spiritual Reading.* Grand Rapids: Eerdmans, 2006.

Pierce, Larry, and Ken Ham. "Are There Gaps in the Genesis Genealogies?" In *The New Answers Book 2*, edited by Ken Ham, 173–182. Green Forest: Master Books, 2008.

RJS. "Genesis 4–5: Biblical Genealogies." *Jesus Creed* (blog), at patheos.com/blogs/jesuscreed/2009/04/14/genesis-4-5-biblical-genealogies-rjs. 14 April 2009.

Ross, Hugh. *The Genesis Question: Scientific Advances and the Accuracy of Genesis*. 2nd edition. Colorado Springs: NavPress, 2001.

Sarfati, Jonathan. "Biblical chronogenealogies." *Journal of Creation* 17, no. 3 (2003): 14–18. Also at creation.com/journal-of-creation-tj-173.

"Star-Spangled Banner and the War of 1812." *Encyclopedia Smithsonian*. At si.edu/Encyclopedia_SI/nmah/starflag.htm.

Stott, John. *Understanding the Bible.* 1972. Revised, Grand Rapids: Zondervan, 1984.

Ussher, James. *Annals of the World*. London: 1658. Also at archive.org/details/AnnalsOfTheWorld.

Waltke, Bruce K, with Charles Yu. *An Old Testament theology: an exegetical, canonical, and thematic approach*. Grand Rapids: Zondervan, 2007.

Walton, John. *Ancient Israelite Literature in its Cultural Context: A Survey of Parallels Between Biblical and Ancient Near Eastern Texts*. Grand Rapids: Zondervan, 1989.

_____. *The NIV Application Commentary: Genesis*. Grand Rapids: Zondervan, 2001.

Wright, N. T. *The Last Word: Scripture and the Authority of God—Getting Beyond the Bible Wars*. New York: HarperCollins, 2005.

8 Optimism

Augustine of Hippo. *On Christian Doctrine*. Translated by Marcus Dods. In vol. 2 of *Nicene and Post-Nicene Fathers of the Christian Church*, 1st series, edited by Philip Schaff. 1887. Reprint, Grand Rapids: Eerdmans, 1988. Also at ccel.org/ccel/schaff/npnf102.

Bube, Richard. *Putting it All Together: Seven Patterns for Relating Science and the Christian Faith*. New York: University Press of America, 1995.

Eddington, Arthur S. "The End of the World: From the Standpoint of Mathematical Physics." *Nature* 127, no. 3203 (1931): 450 and 452. Also at nature.com/articles/127447a0.

Figuier, Louis. *Lives of Illustrious Scholars: from antiquity to the nineteenth century*. Paris: Hachette, 1876. Also at gallica.bnf.fr/ark:/12148/bpt6k96842754 (French).

Galilei, Galileo. *Dialogue on the Two World Systems—Ptolemaic & Copernican*. Translated by Stillman Drake. 2nd edition. Berkeley: University of California Press, 1967.

_____. "Letter to the Grand Duchess Christina." Quoted in *Discoveries and Opinions of Galileo*, edited and translated by Stillman Drake, 173–216. New York: Anchor-Doubleday, 1957.

_____. *The Works of Galileo Galilei, National Edition*. Edited by Antonio Favaro. Florence: Giunti-Barbèra, 1934. Also at portalegalileo. museogalileo.it (Italian).

Gamow, George. "The Evolutionary Universe," *Scientific American* 195, no. 3 (1956): 136–154. Also at scientificamerican.com/magazine/sa/1956/09-01.

Gould, Stephen Jay. *Rocks of Ages: Science and Religion in the Fullness of Life*. New York: Ballantine Books, 1999.

Guenther, D. E. "Electron beam effects on $(CH_2)_{17}$ self-assembled monolayer SiO–Si specimens," *Journal of Vacuum Science Technology A* 12 (1994): 2478–2485. Also at doi.org/10.1116/1.579197.

Guenther, D. E. "The Galileo Affair Revisited." Paper submitted to Regent College, May 2010. At academia.edu/33151519.

Hastings, Ross. *Echoes of Coinherence: Trinitarian Theology and Science Together.* Eugene: Cascade Books, 2017.

Hoyle, Fred. *The Nature of the Universe.* New York: Harper & Brothers, 1950.

Jastrow, Robert. *God and the Astronomers.* 2nd edition. New York: W. W. Norton, 1992.

Lisle, Jason. *Taking Back Astronomy: The Heavens Declare Creation.* Green Forest: Master Books, 2006.

Moreland, J. P. *Christianity and the Nature of Science.* Grand Rapids: Baker Books, 1989.

Opere (Le Opere di Galileo Galilei). See Galilei, Galileo, *The Works of Galileo Galileo, National Edition.*

Origgi, Gloria. "Say goodbye to the information age: it's all about reputation now." *Aeon,* 14 March 2018. At aeon.co/ideas/say-goodbye-to-the-information-age-its-all-about-reputation-now.

Polanyi, Michael. *Personal Knowledge: Towards a Post-Critical Philosophy.* Chicago: University of Chicago Press, 1958.

Ratzsch, Del. *Science and its Limits.* 2nd edition. Downer's Grove: IVP Academic, 2000.

Walton, John. *The Lost World of Genesis One: Ancient Cosmology and the Origins Debate.* Downer's Grove: Intervarsity Press, 2009.

White, Andrew Dickson. *A History of the Warfare of Science with Theology in the History of Christendom.* 1896. Reprint, Buffalo: Prometheus Books, 1993. Also at gutenberg.org/ebooks/505.

Doxology

Bacon, Francis. *The Advancement of Learning.* 1605. Reprint, London: Cassell & Company, 1893. Also at gutenberg.org/files/5500/5500-h/5500-h.htm.

All URLs accessed 01 July 2022. Updated URLs for links in works cited can be found at **EpicScienceAncientFaith.org.**